Introduction

The colorful array of designs in this book will provide inspiration for all kinds of quilting projects, not just pot holders! Use them like you would a collection of 101 blocks—for bed quilts, wall quilts, table runners, holiday decorations or for whatever is your project of the moment. And, of course, use them to make pot holders for gifts and to brighten up your own kitchen.

Contents

General Instructions

With the exception of a few rectangular blocks, most of the block designs given in this book are 8" square. The patterns may be used to make any type of quilted project including bed-size quilts, table runners or wall quilts. Whether you choose to repeat one block design or use a sampler of many, these designs are versatile as well as unique.

The pot holders are grouped in collections. Each collection includes a group photo and block drawings, piecing diagrams and instructions for cutting and assembling each block in the group. You will be referred to these General Instructions for techniques that are repeated often.

Whether you choose to make a few pot holders for yourself or to give as gifts, you are sure to enjoy the satisfaction of completing a project.

Basic Tools & Supplies

Specific fabrics and pieces needed are listed for each pot holder; however there are basic tools, supplies and materials that are needed to finish the pieced blocks into pot holders.

Below is a list of tools and supplies needed for each pot holder:

• Fabrics

Use tightly woven, 100 percent cotton fabric in colors listed or in your own choice of colors for all piecing and appliqué.

Backing Fabric

A 100 percent cotton backing piece should be cut 1" larger all around than the finished block. It can be made of any fabric, but a print that won't show the wear and tear is more practical.

Batting

One layer of regular batting does not work in pot holders. The pot holders in this book each have three layers of cotton batting.

The batting is cut the same size as the backing. You may purchase heat-resistant batting. Insul-Bright is a needle-punched, insulated lining. It is not heat-proof, but it is heat-resistant.

Hanging Ring

A 1" plastic ring is stitched to the top corner of each of the pot holders in this book.

Thread

You will need a neutral color cotton thread for piecing each block. Clear nylon monofilament should not be used in pot holders because it can melt with high heat.

Depending on whether you choose to hand- or machine-quilt the layers together, you will need quilting thread. It may be matching or contrasting, depending on whether you want your stitches to show.

Template Material

Instructions are given for using templates later, but you will need template material to create patterns for cutting pieces.

Fine-Tip Permanent Marker

Use this marker to trace around the templates onto the wrong side of the fabrics.

Fusible Web

Fusible web is a paper-backed fusible product that is applied to the wrong side of appliqué shapes and used to bond the shapes to the fabrics. It is used when machine-appliqué methods are recommended.

Rotary Cutter, Mat & Rotary Ruler

Many of the patterns require strips to be trimmed at an angle. Rotary tools make this type of trimming easy.

Chalk pencil or fine lead pencil

Marking tools are used to trace patterns onto template material and to transfer embroidery or appliqué detail lines to the templates and fabric.

Basic Sewing Tools

Needles, pins, shears, scissors, ruler and other basic sewing tools may be needed.

Basic Technique Instructions

Basic piecing and appliqué techniques are used to complete the pot holders. This simple review of the techniques should help a beginner with questions.

Making Templates

All piecing and appliqué templates are given at the end of the book. They are grouped and labeled by shape; for example, all triangles are labeled with T and a number. All squares are labeled with S and any other shape is labeled M for miscellaneous. If a block requires T12, look for this template with other T pieces.

To create a template, place the template material over the printed page and trace the shape using a fine-tip permanent marker. Transfer the grain-line arrows to the piece. Add the label to the template so that if you have to use it again, you will be able to identify it. It would be a good idea to add a check to the template on the page to indicate you have made a template of the piece.

Place all traced templates together in a folder or envelope and label for future use.

Appliqué pieces are given without seam allowance. If you will be hand-appliquéing the pieces, a ⅛"–¼" seam allowance should be added to fabric pieces when cutting. More detailed appliqué instructions are found in the Appliqué section.

Cutting Fabric for Piecing

Place the prepared template right side down on the wrong side of selected fabric referring to grain-line placement marked on the template as shown in Figure 1; trace around edges using a fine-tip permanent marker referring to project instructions for number and color to cut. Cut out shapes on marked lines.

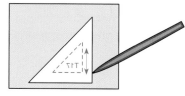

Figure 1

Piecing

Machine-piecing is recommended for all patterns in this book. Set your machine stitch length from 10–12 stitches per inch or 2.5–3.

All seam allowances are ¼" and are included in piecing templates and pieces listed in the cutting instructions provided with each pattern.

To join pieces, pin two pieces right sides together with edges aligned and stitch from one end to the other using a ¼" seam allowance. Secure seams at the beginning and the end, if desired.

Partial Seams

Many of the blocks include adding pieces using partial seams. This method is often used to frame the center or outside of the block. The piece being added may be an unpieced or pieced strip.

To begin a partial seam, match one end of the piece being added to the unit it will be stitched to; stitch along the length to within 1" of the end of the unit being stitched to as shown in Figure 2. Press the seam as directed with the pattern, normally toward the piece being added as shown in Figure 3.

Figure 2

Figure 3

Pin and stitch the second piece being added to the stitched end of the previously stitched unit as shown in Figure 4; press.

Figure 4

Continue adding strips until you reach the starting side with the partial seam; complete sewing the loose end to complete the partial seam as shown in Figure 5 and press.

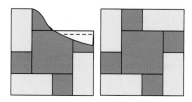

Figure 5

Appliqué

Appliqué shapes are added on top of pieced sections or plain pieces. Most of the appliquéd designs in this book are hand-appliquéd.

Hand-appliquéd pieces are lightly traced on the right side of the fabric using a chalk pencil or fine lead pencil. Cut around traced patterns, adding a ⅛"–¼" seam allowance all around when cutting.

To stitch in place, fold edges under to the marked lines as you stitch the piece to the background using thread to match the fabric referring to Figure 6.

Figure 6

To make curved edges lie flat, cut perpendicular slits into the seam allowance to the marked line as shown in Figure 7.

Figure 7

Using a sharp needle and a 12"–18" length of thread, turn the edge under at the marked line and stitch to the background. Do not turn under edges of pieces where they are overlapped by other pieces.

For fusible machine appliqué, you will need to purchase fusible web. Reverse patterns and trace onto the paper side of the fusible web; then cut out, leaving a margin around each one. Fuse the paper shape to the wrong side of fabrics as directed on patterns for number and color to cut; cut out shapes on traced lines. Remove paper backing.

Arrange the appliqué shape on the background and fuse in place referring to the manufactuer's instructions.

Using a machine zigzag or satin stitch, stitch around the edges of the piece with matching or contrasting thread.

Fabric stabilizer may be used under the stitching area to keep the background from puckering when stitching if desired.

Embroidery

Many of the appliqué shapes have embroidered details. The colors and stitches used are given in the individual pot-holder instructions.

Two strands of embroidery floss are recommended for most embroidered stitches in this book.

Refer to the stitch diagrams given on page 5 for embroidery stitches.

Crazy Patchwork

Crazy patchwork is used to create shapes for some of the pot holders. Scrap patches of fabric are stitched onto a lightweight background of cotton muslin and trimmed to the size needed either using rotary-cutting tools or templates.

Begin with a scrap in the center of the background piece as shown in Figure 8; place a second piece right sides together with this piece and stitch along the aligned edges as shown in Figure 9. Press the top piece to the right side.

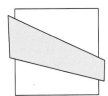

Figure 8

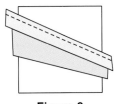

Figure 9

Continue adding scrap pieces around the center to completely cover the background fabric and all raw edges of the scraps as shown in Figure 10.

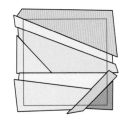

Figure 10

Finishing the Pot Holders

Layer a completed block with a backing and batting square or rectangle 1" larger all around; pin or baste layers together to hold flat.

Quilt by hand or machine using quilting thread to match or contrast with fabrics. Most of the pot holders in this book were machine-quilted in the ditch of seams between the pieces.

When quilting is complete, trim the batting and backing edges even with the pieced block.

A length and color suggestion for the binding is listed with each pot holder design. Press this length of binding in half along the length with wrong sides together to make a double-layered strip.

Pin the raw edge of the binding strip to the raw edge of the right side of the pot holder, leaving 4" at the beginning loose as shown in Figure 11.

Figure 11

Stitch to within ¼" of one corner; leaving the needle in the fabric, turn and sew diagonally to the corner as shown in Figure 12.

Figure 12

American School of Needlework • Berne, Indiana 46711 • DRGnetwork.com

Fold the binding at a 45-degree angle up and away from the pot holder as shown in Figure 13 and back down even with the raw edge of the next side.

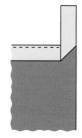

Figure 13

Starting at the top raw edge of the pot holder, begin sewing the next side as shown in Figure 14. Repeat at the next three corners.

Figure 14

As you approach the beginning of the binding strip, stop stitching and overlap the binding ends ½" as shown in Figure 15; trim. Join the two ends with a ¼" seam allowance and press the seam open. Reposition the joined binding strip along the edge and resume stitching to the beginning.

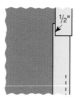

Figure 15

Press the binding strip up and away from the pot holder on the right side; turn to the back side and hand-stitch in place, mitering the corners on the back side as shown in Figure 16.

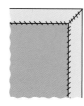

Figure 16

Add Hanging Ring

Hand-stitch a 1" plastic ring to one corner of your finished pot holder for hanging, if desired.

Embroidery Stitches

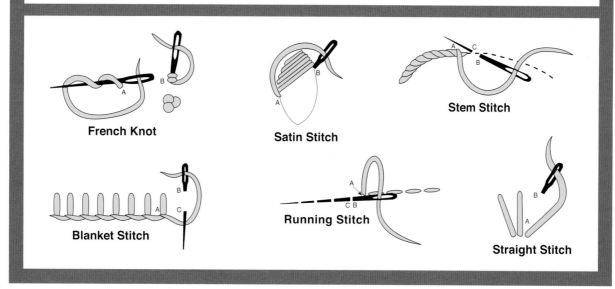

French Knot

Satin Stitch

Stem Stitch

Blanket Stitch

Running Stitch

Straight Stitch

Through the Window

Make a set of pot holders with a stained glass look using blue and yellow fabrics.

Project Notes

Cut pieces as listed either using a rotary cutter and rotary ruler or the templates from those starting on page 87.

Refer to the General Instructions for a list of basic sewing supplies and tools needed and for instructions to finish your pot holders.

Refer to the Piecing Diagram given with each block for assembly ideas.

Sun & Sky

Fabric & Piece Requirements

- 2 S3 yellow solid
- 3 S3 cream print
- 4 S3 turquoise print
- 6 - 1" x 2½" A purple print
- 2 - 1" x 7½" B purple print
- 4 - 1" x 8" C purple print
- 1 - 2" x 36" strip gold print for binding

Instructions

1. Arrange and join the S3 squares with A in three rows of three squares each; press seams toward A.

2. Join the rows with B; press seams toward B to complete the pieced center.

3. Sew C to each side of the pieced center using a partial seam referring to the General Instructions to complete the pieced block.

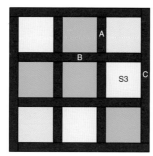

Sun & Sky
Placement Diagram
8" x 8"

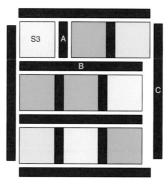

Piecing Diagram

Windowpanes

Fabric & Piece Requirements

- 18 S9 each purple and turquoise prints
- 6 - 1" x 2½" A lavender tonal
- 2 - 1" x 7½" B lavender tonal
- 4 - 1" x 8" C lavender tonal
- 1 - 2" x 36" strip green print for binding

Instructions

1. Sew a turquoise S9 to a purple S9; press seams toward darker fabric. Repeat to make 18 S9 units.

2. Join two S9 units to make a Four-Patch unit referring to Figure 1; press seam in one direction. Repeat to make nine Four-Patch units.

Figure 1

3. Join three Four-Patch units with two A pieces to make a row; press seams toward A. Repeat to make three rows.

4. Join the rows with B; press seams toward B to complete the pieced center.

5. Sew C to each side of the pieced center using partial seams referring to the General Instructions to complete the pieced block.

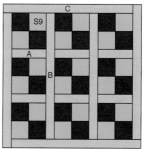

Windowpanes
Placement Diagram
8" x 8"

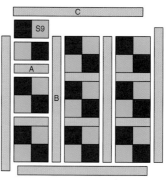

Piecing Diagram

Afternoon Shadows

Fabric & Piece Requirements
- 9 T18 triangles each lavender tonal and purple print
- 6 - 1" x 2½" A cream tonal
- 2 - 1" x 7½" B cream tonal
- 4 - 1" x 8" C cream tonal
- 1 - 2" x 36" strip green print for binding

Instructions
1. Sew a lavender T18 to a purple T18 along the diagonal; press seams toward darker fabric. Repeat to make nine T18 units.
2. Join three T18 units with two A pieces to make a row; press seams toward A. Repeat to make three rows.
3. Join the rows with B; press seams toward B to complete the pieced center.
4. Sew C to each side of the pieced center using partial seams referring to the General Instructions to complete the pieced block.

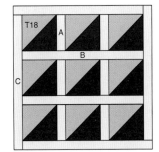

Afternoon Shadows
Placement Diagram
8" x 8"

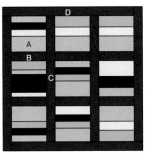

Piecing Diagram

West Winds

Fabric & Piece Requirements
- Assorted coordinating scraps cut into 3"-long strips in varying widths from ½"–1½" wide
- 6 - 1" x 2½" B purple print
- 2 - 1" x 7½" C purple print
- 4 - 1" x 8" D purple print
- 1 - 2" x 36" strip blue print for binding

Instructions
1. Referring to Figure 2, join a variety of scrap strips and square to 3" x 3" to make a scrappy A square; press seams in one direction. Repeat to make nine scrappy A squares.
2. Referring to Figure 3, join three scrappy A squares with two B pieces to make a row; press seams toward B. Repeat to make three rows.

Figure 2

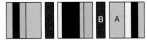

Figure 3

3. Join the rows with C; press seams toward C to complete the pieced center.
4. Sew D to each side of the pieced center using partial seams referring to the General Instructions to complete the pieced block.

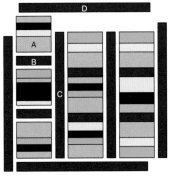

West Winds
Placement Diagram
8" x 8"

Piecing Diagram

Bluebird Quartet

Fabric & Piece Requirements
- 2 S3 each blue mottled and turquoise print
- 8 S9 each blue mottled and turquoise print
- 16 - 1½" x 2½" A yellow print
- 1 - 2" x 36" strip yellow print for binding

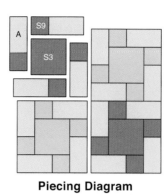

Piecing Diagram

Figure 6

3. Join two S3 units to make a Four-Patch unit referring to Figure 7; press seam in one direction. Repeat to make two Four-Patch units.

Figure 7

Instructions

1. Sew a blue S9 square to A to make an A-S9 unit; press seam toward A. Repeat to make eight each blue and turquoise A-S9 units.

2. Match the S9 end of an A-S9 unit to one end of a matching S3 square and stitch to within 1" of the end of S3 to make a partial seam as shown in Figure 4; press seam away from S3.

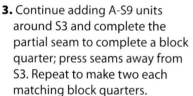

Figure 4

3. Continue adding A-S9 units around S3 and complete the partial seam to complete a block quarter; press seams away from S3. Repeat to make two each matching block quarters.

4. Join one each-color block quarter to make a row; press seams toward blue block quarters. Repeat to make two rows.

5. Join the rows to complete the pieced block.

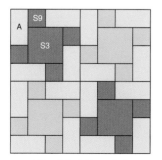

Bluebird Quartet
Placement Diagram
8" x 8"

Lovebirds

Fabric & Piece Requirements
• 2 S3 blue mottled
• 4 S3 each lavender and gold solids
• 8 S9 blue mottled
• 8 - 1½" x 2½" A yellow print
• 1 - 2" x 36" strip yellow print for binding

Instructions

1. Complete two blue mottled block quarters referring to Figures 4 and 5 and Steps 1–3 for Bluebird Quartet.

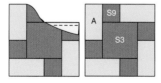

Figure 5

2. Sew a lavender S3 to a gold S3 to make an S3 unit referring to Figure 6; press seam toward darker fabric. Repeat to make four S3 units.

4. Join one Four-Patch unit and one block quarter to make a row; press seams toward the Four-Patch unit. Repeat to make two rows.

5. Join the rows to complete the pieced block.

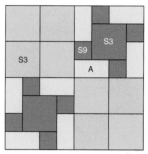

Lovebirds
Placement Diagram
8" x 8"

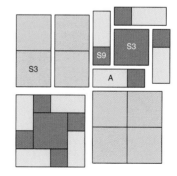

Piecing Diagram

Creative Cook

Many quilt blocks have a food-related name, which makes them perfect designs for use when making pot holders.

Project Notes

Cut pieces as listed either using a rotary cutter and rotary ruler or the templates from those starting on page 87.

Refer to the General Instructions for a list of basic sewing supplies and tools needed and for instructions to finish your pot holders.

Refer to the Piecing Diagram given with each block for assembly ideas.

Sunny-Side Up

Fabric & Piece Requirements

• 2 S1 peach mottled
• 32 S9 assorted fabrics
• 1 - 2" x 36" strip cream print for binding

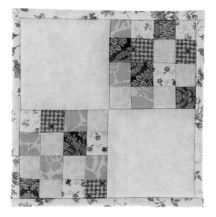

Instructions

1. Join four S9 squares to make a row; repeat to make eight rows. Press seams in one direction.
2. Join four S9 rows to make an S9 unit, alternating direction of seams in rows; press seams in one direction. Repeat to make two S9 units.
3. Sew an S9 unit to S1 to make a row; press seam toward S1. Repeat to make two rows.
4. Join the rows to complete the pieced top; press seam in one direction.

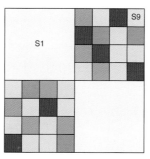

Sunny-Side Up
Placement Diagram
8" x 8"

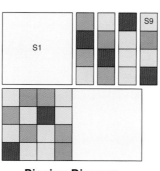

Piecing Diagram

Dessert Party

Fabric & Piece Requirements

• 2 S1 cream print
• 2 S3 rose print
• 8 S9 rose print
• 8 - 1½" x 2½" A pink tonal
• 1 - 2" x 36" strip tan print for binding

Instructions

1. Sew S9 to opposite ends of A; repeat to make four S9-A units. Press seams toward S9.
2. Sew A to opposite sides of S3; press seams toward S3. Repeat to make two S3-A units.
3. Sew an S9-A unit to opposite sides of an S3-A unit to complete an A-S unit; press seams toward the S3-A unit. Repeat to make two A-S units.

4. Sew S1 to an A-S unit to make a row; press seam toward S1. Repeat to make two row units. Join the rows to complete the pieced top; press seam in one direction.

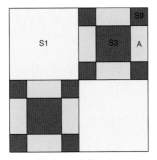

Dessert Party
Placement Diagram
8" x 8"

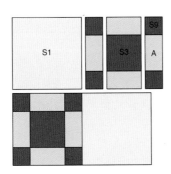

Piecing Diagram

Pink Lemonade

Fabric & Piece Requirements
• 16 S9 pink tonal
• 20 S9 green print
• 1 S3 green leaf print
• 4 S3 cream tonal
• 4 - 1½" x 2½" A pink tonal
• 20" length ½"-wide pink rickrack
• 1 - 2" x 36" strip gold print for binding

Instructions
1. Referring to Figure 1, sew a pink S9 between two green S9's; press seams toward the center square. Repeat to make eight units.

Make 8

Make 4

Figure 1

2. Sew a green S9 between two pink S9's, again referring to Figure 1; press seams away from the center square. Repeat to make four units.

3. Sew a pink/green/pink S9 unit between two green/pink/green S9 units to complete a Nine-Patch unit as shown in Figure 2; press seams toward the center unit. Repeat to make four Nine-Patch units.

Figure 2

4. Sew A to opposite sides of the green S3; press seams toward A. Add a cream S3 to each A side to complete the center row; press seams toward S3.

5. Sew A to one end of each remaining cream S3 to make two side units; press seams toward A.

6. Sew a side unit between two Nine-Patch units to make a side row; press seams toward the side unit. Repeat to make two side rows.

7. Sew the center row between the two side rows; press seams toward the center row.

8. Cut the pink rickrack into four 5" pieces.

9. Unpick the seams between the center green and inside pink S9 squares as shown in Figure 3.

Figure 3

10. Insert a piece of rickrack into the seam between units all around as shown in Figure 4; when satisfied with placement, stitch rickrack in place.

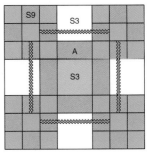

Figure 4

11. Re-stitch seams to complete the pieced top.

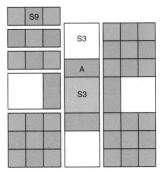

Pink Lemonade
Placement Diagram
8" x 8"

Piecing Diagram

Supper Time

Fabric & Piece Requirements
- 1 S3 each pink and orange tonals and green and purple prints
- 4 S3 cream tonal
- 2 S9 each cream solid and cream print
- 5 S9 each pink and orange tonals and green and purple prints
- 8 S9 cream tonal
- 1 - 2" x 36" strip peach print for binding

Instructions
1. Sew a pink S9 to a cream tonal S9; press seam toward darker fabric. Repeat to make two units; add a pink S9 to the cream end of one unit; press seams toward darker fabric.

2. Sew the pink/cream S9 to one side of the pink S3; press seam toward S3. Sew the pink/cream/pink S9 unit to the adjacent side of S3 to complete a corner unit as shown in Figure 5; press seams away from S3.

Figure 5

3. Repeat step 2 to make one each purple, green and orange corner unit.

4. Sew a pink S9 to a green S9 to make a pink/green unit; repeat to make one each pink/purple, orange/purple and green/orange units; press seams toward darker fabrics.

5. Sew these units to one end of each cream S3 to make side units as shown in Figure 6; press seams toward S3.

Figure 6

6. Sew a cream solid S9 to a cream print S9; repeat. Press seams toward the print square. Join the two units to complete the center unit; press seam in one direction.

7. Arrange and join the pieced units in rows referring to the Piecing Diagram; press seams in one direction.

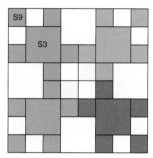

Supper Time
Placement Diagram
8" x 8"

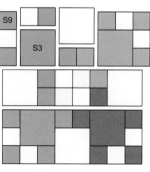

Piecing Diagram

Biscuit Baskets

Fabric & Piece Requirements
- 2 T4 each purple, green and rose prints and orange tonal
- 20 T4 purple mottled
- 28 T4 pink tonal
- 1 S3 each purple, green and rose prints and orange tonal
- 5 S3 pink tonal
- 1 - 2" x 36" strip white print for binding

Instructions
1. Sew a pink T4 to each remaining T4 to make T units; press seams away from the pink T4 triangles.

2. Join two pink/purple T units as shown in Figure 7; press seam in one direction. Repeat to make four units.

3. Sew a unit to one side of each orange, green, pumpkin and rose S3 square; press seams toward S3.

4. Join three pink/purple T units, again referring to Figure 7; press seams in one direction. Repeat to make four units.

Make 4

Make 4

T4

Figure 7

5. Sew a unit to the adjacent sides of the previously pieced unit to complete the corner units as shown in Figure 8; press seams toward S3.

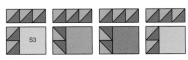

Figure 8

6. Join the remaining T units with pink sides touching as shown in Figure 9; press seams open. Sew these units to pink S3 squares, again referring to Figure 9; press seams toward S3.

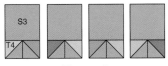

Figure 9

7. Arrange and join the pieced units in rows referring to the Piecing Diagram; press seams in adjacent rows in opposite directions.

8. Join the rows to complete the pieced top; press seams in one direction.

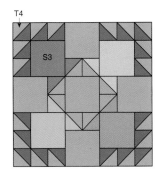

Biscuit Baskets
Placement Diagram
8" x 8"

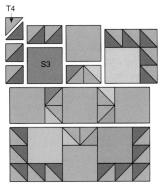

Piecing Diagram

Town Square

Center units are framed with triangles or strips in these colorful pot holders.

Project Notes
Cut pieces as listed either using a rotary cutter and rotary ruler or the templates from those starting on page 87.

Refer to the General Instructions for a list of basic sewing supplies and tools needed and for instructions to finish your pot holders.

Refer to the Piecing Diagram given with each block for assembly ideas.

Evening Walk

Fabric & Piece Requirements
- 2 S12 each green tonal and blue solid
- 4 T22 tan tonal
- 4 - 1¾" x 7" A navy print
- 4 - 1¼" x 5¾" B red print
- 4 - 1" x 5¾" C green solid
- 1 - 2" x 36" strip burgundy solid for binding

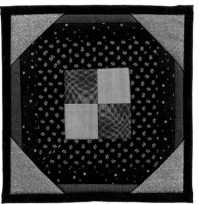

American School of Needlework • Berne, Indiana 46711 • DRGnetwork.com

Instructions

1. Sew a blue S12 to a green S 12; repeat. Press seam toward darker fabric.

2. Join the two S12 units to complete the block center as shown in Figure 1; press seam in one direction.

Figure 1

3. Center and sew an A strip on each side of the block center, mitering corners; press seams toward A. ***Note:*** *Refer to the General Instructions for making mitered corner seams.*

4. Sew a B strip to a C strip; press seam toward C. Repeat to make four B-C strips.

5. Trim each end of the B-C strips at a 45-degree angle as shown in Figure 2.

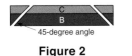

Figure 2

6. Sew a trimmed strip to each side of the pieced center.

7. Sew T22 to each corner to complete the block; press seams toward T22.

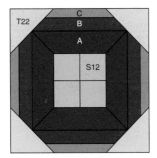

Evening Walk
Placement Diagram
8" x 8"

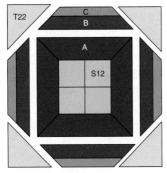

Piecing Diagram

Green Space

Fabric & Piece Requirements
- 2 S12 each green tonal and blue solid
- 4 T22 red print
- 4 - 1¼" x 6" A yellow print
- 4 - 1¼" x 5¾" B green solid
- 4 - 1½" x 6½" C pumpkin solid
- 1 - 2" x 36" strip burgundy solid for binding

Instructions

1. Sew a blue S12 to a green S12; repeat. Press seams toward darker fabric.

2. Join the two S12 units to complete the block center, again referring to Figure 1; press seam in one direction.

3. Center and sew an A strip on each side of the block center, mitering corners; press seams toward A. ***Note:*** *Refer to the General Instructions for making mitered corner seams.*

4. Sew a B strip to each side using a partial seam referring to the General Instructions; press seams toward B.

5. Center and sew a C strip to T22 as shown in Figure 3; press seam toward T22. Trim C even with edges of T22, again referring to Figure 3. Repeat to make four C-T22 units.

Figure 3

6. Sew a C-T22 unit to each side of the pieced unit; press seams toward the C-T22 units.

7. Trim the B strips even with the edges of the C-T22 units to complete the block as shown in Figure 4.

Figure 4

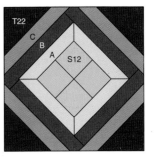

Green Space
Placement Diagram
8" x 8"

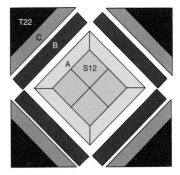

Piecing Diagram

Brass Band

Fabric & Piece Requirements
- 2 S5 each red and white/red prints
- 4 T29 each cream tonal and tan print
- 4 T19 black print
- 4 - 2⅝" x 4" A black check
- 1 - 2" x 36" strip burgundy tonal for binding

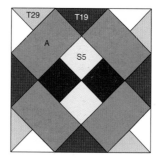

Brass Band
Placement Diagram
8" x 8"

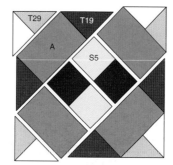

Piecing Diagram

Instructions

1. Sew a red S5 to a white/red S5; press seam toward darker fabric. Repeat to make two units.

2. Join the two S5 units to complete the center unit; press seam in one direction.

3. Sew T19 to each end of A; press seam toward T19. Repeat to make two A-T19 units.

4. Sew a cream T29 to a tan T29; press seam toward darker fabric. Repeat to make four T29 units.

5. Sew a T29 unit to an A-T19 unit to complete a corner unit as shown in Figure 5; press seam toward the T29 unit. Repeat to make two corner units.

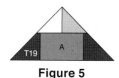

Figure 5

6. Sew A to opposite sides of the S5 center unit; press seams toward A. Add a T29 unit to each A end to complete the center row referring to Figure 6; press seams toward A.

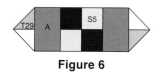

Figure 6

7. Sew a corner unit to opposite sides of the center row to complete the pieced block; press seams toward corner units.

Town Fathers

Fabric & Piece Requirements

- 2 T3 each red print and green solid
- 4 - 2¼" x 5" A yellow print
- 4 - 2¼" x 5" B black print
- 1 - 2" x 36" strip black dot for binding

Instructions

1. Sew a red T3 to a green T3 as shown in Figure 7; press seam toward the darker fabric. Repeat to make two T3 units.

Figure 7

2. Join the T3 units as shown in Figure 8 to complete the block center; press seam in one direction.

Figure 8

3. Sew A to B on the short ends; press seam toward the darker fabric. Repeat to make four A-B units.

4. Center and sew an A-B unit to each side of the block center, mitering corners referring to the General Instructions to complete the pieced block.

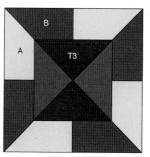

Town Fathers
Placement Diagram
8" x 8"

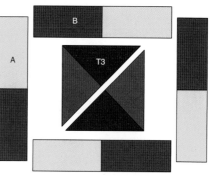

Piecing Diagram

Bright Ideas

Bright colors, especially yellow, stand out in these pot holders with framed centers.

Project Notes

Cut pieces as listed either using a rotary cutter and rotary ruler or the templates from those starting on page 87.

Refer to the General Instructions for a list of basic sewing supplies and tools needed and for instructions to finish your pot holders.

Refer to the Piecing Diagram given with each block for assembly ideas.

Lilac Square

Fabric & Piece Requirements

- 1 S2 lavender solid
- 4 S13 purple tonal
- 4 T18 rust tonal
- 4 - 1¼" x 4½" A aqua solid
- 2 - 1" x 6" B cream tonal
- 2 - 1" x 7" C cream tonal
- 2 - 1¼" x 7" D yellow dot
- 2 - 1¼" x 8½" E yellow dot
- 1 - 2" x 36" strip red print for binding

Instructions

1. Sew T18 to each side of S2 to complete the block center; press seams toward T18.
2. Sew A to opposite sides of the block center; press seams toward A.
3. Sew S13 to each end of each remaining A; press seams toward A.
4. Sew an A-S13 unit to the remaining sides of the block center; press seams toward A-S13.
5. Sew B to opposite sides and C to the remaining sides of the block center; press seams toward B and C. Repeat with D and E strips to complete the pieced block.

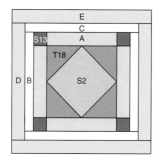

Lilac Square
Placement Diagram
8" x 8"

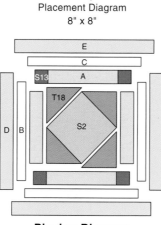

Piecing Diagram

Royal Blue Square

Fabric & Piece Requirements

- 1 S2 bright blue tonal
- 8 S9 each yellow dot and black print
- 4 T18 lavender solid
- 4 - 1½" x 4½" A fuchsia solid
- 4 - 1½" x 4½" B cream/purple print
- 1 - 2" x 36" strip gold solid for binding

Instructions

1. Sew T18 to each side of S2 to complete the block center; press seams toward T18.
2. Sew a yellow S9 to a black S9; press seam toward the darker fabric. Repeat to make eight S9 units.
3. Join two S9 units to make a corner unit; press seam in one direction. Repeat to make four corner units.

4. Sew A to B along the length; press seam toward B. Repeat to make four A-B units.

5. Sew an A-B unit to opposite sides of the block center; press seams toward A-B.

6. Sew a corner unit to each end of each remaining A-B unit; press seams toward A-B.

7. Sew an A-B/corner unit to the remaining sides of the block center to complete the pieced block; press seams away from the block center.

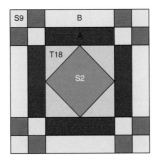

Royal Blue Square
Placement Diagram
8" x 8"

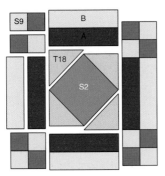

Piecing Diagram

Blood Orange Square

Fabric & Piece Requirements
- 1 S2 coral print
- 8 S9 each lavender solid and coral print
- 4 S3 orange tonal
- 4 - 1½" x 4½" A yellow dot
- 1 - 2" x 36" strip gold solid for binding

Instructions
1. Sew T18 to each side of S2 to complete the block center; press seams toward T18.

2. Join two each lavender and coral S9 squares to make an S9 strip; press seams toward darker fabric. Repeat to make four S9 strips.

3. Sew an S9 strip to A; press seam toward A. Repeat to make four A-S9 strips.

4. Sew an A-S9 strip to opposite sides of the block center; press seams toward the A-S9 strip.

5. Sew an S3 square to each end of each remaining A-S9 strip; press seams toward S3.

6. Sew the pieced strips to the remaining sides of the block center to complete the pieced block; press seams away from the block center.

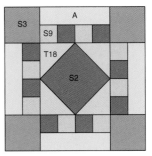

Blood Orange Square
Placement Diagram
8" x 8"

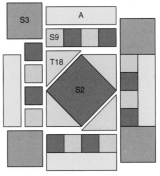

Piecing Diagram

X-tra X-tra

Fabric & Piece Requirements
- 1 S12 coral print
- 4 S3 orange solid
- 4 - 2" x 2½" A blue check
- 2 - 1" x 6" B yellow dot
- 2 - 1" x 7" C yellow dot
- 2 - 1¼" x 7" D turquoise print
- 2 - 1¼" x 8½" E turquoise print
- 1 - 2" x 36" strip gold solid for binding

Instructions

1. Sew A to opposite sides of S12 to make the center row; press seams toward A.

2. Sew A between two S3 squares; press seams toward A. Repeat to make two A-S3 rows.

3. Sew an A-S3 row to opposite sides of the center row; press seams toward the A-S3 rows.

4. Sew B and then C to the sides of the pieced center; press seams toward B and C.

5. Sew D and then E to the sides of the pieced center to complete the pieced block; press seams toward D and E.

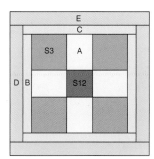

X-tra X-tra
Placement Diagram
8" x 8"

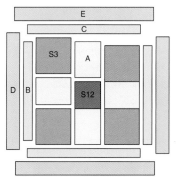

Piecing Diagram

Inspiration

Fabric & Piece Requirements
- 1 S12 blue solid
- 8 T4 lavender solid
- 4 M12 royal blue tonal
- 4 - 2" x 2½" A coral print
- 2 - 1" x 6" B red print
- 2 - 1" x 7" C red print
- 2 - 1¼" x 7" D blue check
- 2 - 1¼" x 8½" E blue check
- 1 - 2" x 36" strip red tonal for binding

Instructions

1. Sew A to opposite sides of S12 to complete the center row; press seams toward A.

2. Sew T4 to opposite sides of M12 to make an M-T unit; press seams toward T4. Repeat to make four M-T units.

3. Join two M-T units with A to make a side row; press seams toward A. Repeat to make two side rows.

4. Sew a side row to opposite sides of the center row; press seams toward the center row.

5. Sew B and then C to the sides of the pieced center; press seams toward B and C.

6. Sew D and then E to the sides of the pieced center to complete the pieced block; press seams toward D and E.

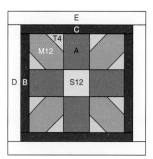

Inspiration
Placement Diagram
8" x 8"

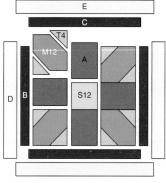

Piecing Diagram

Hot Cross Bun

Fabric & Piece Requirements
- 1 S12 dark red print
- 8 T4 yellow dot
- 4 M12 lavender solid
- 4 - 2" x 2½" A red print
- 2 - 1" x 6" B royal blue tonal
- 2 - 1" x 7" C royal blue tonal
- 2 - 1¼" x 7" D orange tonal
- 2 - 1¼" x 8½" E orange tonal
- 1 - 2" x 36" strip red print for binding

Instructions

1. Piece referring to the instructions for Inspiration and to the Piecing Diagram for Hot Cross Bun to complete the pieced block.

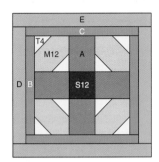

Hot Cross Bun
Placement Diagram
8" x 8"

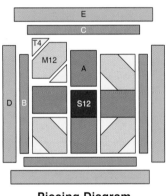

Piecing Diagram

Blue Cross

Fabric & Piece Requirements
- 4 S13 yellow print
- 4 M12 blue solid
- 8 T4 yellow print
- 4 - 1¼" x 4½" A coral print
- 2 - 1" x 6" B purple print
- 2 - 1" x 7" C purple print
- 2 - 1¼" x 7" D rust stripe
- 2 - 1¼" x 8½" E rust stripe
- 1 - 2" x 36" strip gold solid for binding

Instructions

1. Sew T4 to opposite sides of M12 to make an M-T unit; press seams toward T4. Repeat to make four M-T units.

2. Join two M-T units as shown in Figure 1; press seam in one direction. Repeat to make two units.

Figure 1

3. Join the M-T units to complete the block center; press seam in one direction.

4. Sew A to opposite sides of the block center; press seams toward A.

5. Sew S13 to each end of each remaining A; press seams toward A.

6. Sew an A-S13 unit to the remaining sides of the block center; press seams toward A-S13.

7. Sew B and then C to the sides of the pieced center; press seams toward B and C.

8. Sew D and then E to the sides of the pieced center to complete the pieced block; press seams toward D and E.

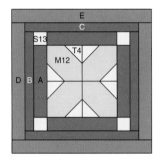

Blue Cross
Placement Diagram
8" x 8"

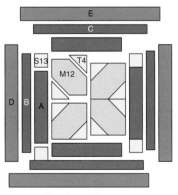

Piecing Diagram

 American School of Needlework • Berne, Indiana 46711 • DRGnetwork.com

All in a Row

Whether diagonal or straight up and down, the units in this set of pot holders are set together in rows.

Project Notes

Cut pieces as listed either using a rotary cutter and rotary ruler or the templates from those starting on page 87.

Refer to the General Instructions for a list of basic sewing supplies and tools needed and for instructions to finish your pot holders.

Refer to the Piecing Diagram given with each block for assembly ideas.

Vegetable Patch

Fabric & Piece Requirements

- Assorted coordinating scraps cut into 3"-long strips in varying widths from ½"–1½" wide for A
- 2 T18 each tan and black prints
- 4 T18 olive solid
- 8 S9 each olive solid and light olive tonal
- 4 - 1" x 8½" B red print
- 1 - 2" x 36" strip gold print for binding

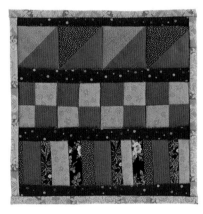

Instructions

1. Referring to Figure 1, join a variety of scrap strips to make an A row; trim the A row to 2½" x 8½".

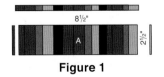

Figure 1

2. Sew an olive solid S9 to a light olive tonal S9 to make an S9 unit; press seam toward darker fabric. Repeat to make eight S9 units.

3. Join the S9 units to make an S9 row referring to Figure 2; press seams in one direction.

Figure 2

4. Sew an olive T18 to a black T18 to make a black T18 unit; press seam toward darker fabric. Repeat to make two black T18 units and two tan units.

5. Join the T18 units to make a row, alternating colors; press seams in one direction.

6. Join the A row with the S9 and T18 rows and B to complete the pieced top.

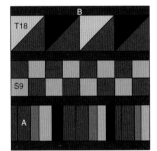

Vegetable Patch
Placement Diagram
8" x 8"

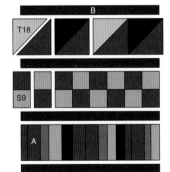

Piecing Diagram

Fall Harvest

Fabric & Piece Requirements

- Assorted coordinating scraps cut into 3"-long strips in varying widths from ½"–1½" wide for A
- 8 T1 each pumpkin and gold solids
- 8 T4 pumpkin solid
- 4 M12 geranium print
- 4 - 1" x 8½" B black print
- 1 - 2" x 36" strip gold print for binding

Instructions

1. Join a variety of scrap strips to make an A row; trim the A row to 2½" x 8½", again referring to Figure 1.

2. Join one gold and one pumpkin T1 as shown in Figure 3; press seam toward darker fabric. Repeat to make eight units. Join two units to make a T1 unit, again referring to Figure 3; press seam in one direction.

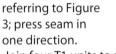

Figure 3

3. Join four T1 units to make a T1 row; press seams in one direction.

4. Sew T4 to opposite sides of M12; press seams toward T4. Repeat to make four M-T units.

5. Join the four M-T units to make a row; press seams in one direction.

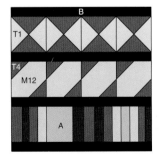

Fall Harvest
Placement Diagram
8" x 8"

6. Join the rows with B to complete the pieced top; press seams toward B.

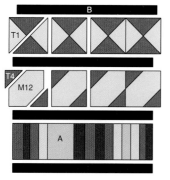

Piecing Diagram

Pumpkin Patch

Fabric & Piece Requirements
- 5 S9 each rose print and burgundy solid
- 6 S9 green dot
- 16 S9 orange tonal
- 2 M12 each burgundy solid and rose print
- 4 M12 green dot
- 16 T4 orange tonal
- 1 - 2" x 36" strip burgundy print for binding

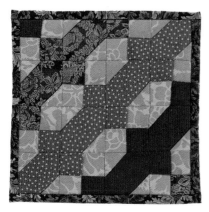

Instructions
1. Sew T4 to opposite sides of each M12 to make an M-T unit; press seams toward T4.

2. Sew a rose S9 to an orange S9 to make a rose S9 unit; press seams toward the darker fabric. Repeat to make five rose S9 units, five burgundy S9 units and six green S9 units.

3. Join the S9 units to make Four-Patch units referring to Figure 4; press seams in one direction.

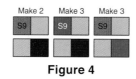

Figure 4

4. Arrange and join the pieced units in rows referring to the Piecing Diagram to complete the pieced top.

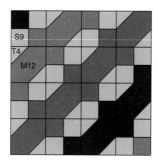

Pumpkin Patch
Placement Diagram
8" x 8"

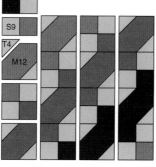

Piecing Diagram

Stepping-Stones

Fabric & Piece Requirements
- 16 T4 each green tonal and gray print
- 8 T18 each yellow and black prints
- 4 S4 each cream tonal and burgundy solid
- 1 - 2" x 36" strip cream print for binding

Instructions
1. Sew a yellow T18 to a black T18 to make a T18 unit; press seams toward darker fabric. Repeat to make eight T18 units.

2. Sew a green T4 to each side of a cream S4 to complete a green/cream S-T unit; press seams toward T4. Repeat to make four green/cream and four gray/burgundy S-T units.

3. Arrange and join the pieced units in rows referring to the Piecing Diagram; press seams in one direction.

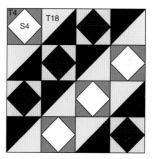

Stepping-Stones
Placement Diagram
8" x 8"

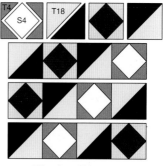

Piecing Diagram

Rays of Sunshine

Bright yellow creates the sunshine in the blue sky for these two pretty pot holders.

Project Notes

Cut pieces as listed either using a rotary cutter and rotary ruler or the templates from those starting on page 87.

Refer to the General Instructions for a list of basic sewing supplies and tools needed and for instructions to finish your pot holders.

Refer to the Piecing Diagram given with each block for assembly ideas.

High Noon

Fabric & Piece Requirements

• 4 S3 blue print
• 8 T4 blue print
• 8 T18 each blue print and dark gold tonal
• 4 M12 light gold tonal
• 1 - 2" x 36" strip tan tonal for binding

Instructions

1. Sew T4 to opposite sides of M12; press seams toward T4. Repeat to make four M-T units.

2. Join two M-T units as shown in Figure 1; press seam in one direction.

Figure 1

Repeat to make two units.

3. Sew a gold T18 to a blue T18; press seam toward the darker fabric; repeat to make eight T18 units.

4. Sew a T18 unit to opposite ends of the joined M-T units to make a row; press seams toward T18 units. Repeat to make two rows.

5. Join two T18 units as shown in Figure 2; press seam in one direction. Repeat to make two units.

Figure 2

6. Sew S3 to opposite ends of each joined T18 unit to complete a side row; press seams toward S3. Repeat to make two side rows.

7. Arrange and join the rows referring to the Piecing Diagram to complete the pieced block; press seams toward the side rows.

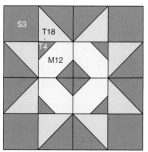

High Noon
Placement Diagram
8" x 8"

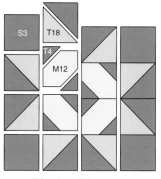

Piecing Diagram

Warm Hug

Fabric & Piece Requirements
- 4 T4 orange tonal
- 8 T4 bright blue tonal
- 4 M12 orange tonal
- 4 M5 bright blue tonal
- 4 - 1" x 2½" B each turquoise and white/purple prints, lavender solid and turquoise check
- 8 - 1½" x 2½" A turquoise print
- 1 - 2" x 36" strip tan tonal for binding

Instructions
1. Sew T4 to opposite sides of M12; press seams toward T4. Repeat to make four M-T units.

2. Join two M-T units referring to Figure 3; press seam in one direction. Repeat to make two M-T rows.

Figure 3

3. Join the M-T rows to complete the block center; press seam in one direction.

4. Join one each fabric B strip to make a B square as shown in Figure 4; press seams in one direction. Repeat to make four B squares.

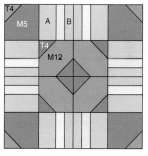

Figure 4

5. Sew A to opposite sides of each B square; press seams toward A.

6. Sew an A-B unit to opposite sides of the block center to complete the center row; press seams toward A-B.

7. Sew T4 to M5 to make a corner unit; press seam toward T4. Repeat to make four corner units.

8. Sew a corner unit to each end of each remaining A-B unit; press seams toward A-B.

9. Sew the corner/A-B strips to the remaining sides of the center row to complete the pieced block; press seams away from the center row.

Warm Hug
Placement Diagram
8" x 8"

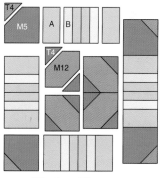

Piecing Diagram

Checkered Past

Lots of squares combine to make Four-Patch and Nine-Patch units in these checkered blocks.

Project Notes

Cut pieces as listed either using a rotary cutter and rotary ruler or the templates from those starting on page 87.

Refer to the General Instructions for a list of basic sewing supplies and tools needed and for instructions to finish your pot holders.

Refer to the Piecing Diagram given with each block for assembly ideas.

Pairings

Fabric & Piece Requirements
- 8 S10 each green print and brown solid
- 10 S10 each blue and cream mottleds
- 4 - ¾" x 8¼" A gold solid
- 1 - 2" x 36" strip burgundy print for binding

Instructions

1. Sew a blue S10 to a cream S10; repeat to make 10 blue S10 units. Press seams toward blue pieces.
2. Join two S10 units to complete a blue Four-Patch unit; press seam in one direction. Repeat to make five blue units.
3. Sew a green S10 to a brown S10 to make a brown S10 unit; repeat to make eight units. Press seams toward brown pieces.
4. Join two S10 units to complete a brown Four-Patch unit; press seam in one direction. Repeat to make four brown units.
5. Arrange and join the Four-Patch units in rows referring to the Piecing Diagram; press seams toward the brown units.
6. Join the rows; press seams away from the center row.
7. Add A to each side of the pieced center using partial seams referring to the General Instructions to complete the pieced block.

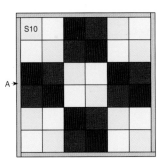

Pairings
Placement Diagram
8" x 8"

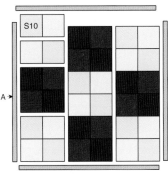

Piecing Diagram

Wild Oats

Fabric & Piece Requirements
- 4 S10 each blue mottled and gold solid
- 5 S10 cream mottled
- 4 - 1¾" x 4¼" A brown solid
- 4 - 1½" x 7½" B gold solid
- 1 - 2" x 36" strip green tonal for binding

American School of Needlework • Berne, Indiana 46711 • DRGnetwork.com

Instructions

1. Sew a blue S10 between two cream S10's to make a row; press seam toward the blue piece. Repeat to make two rows.

2. Sew a cream S10 between two blue S10's to make the center row; press seams toward the blue pieces.

3. Join the rows referring to the Piecing Diagram to complete the block center; press seams away from the center row.

4. Sew A to opposite sides of the block center; press seams toward A.

5. Sew a gold S10 to each end of each remaining A; press seams toward A.

6. Sew an A-S10 unit to the remaining sides of the block center; press seams toward A-S10.

7. Sew B to each side of the pieced center using partial seams referring to the General Instructions to complete the pieced block.

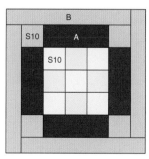

Wild Oats
Placement Diagram
8" x 8"

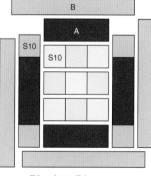

Piecing Diagram

English Garden

Blocks with flower colors create a fabric garden in these ladylike pot holders.

Project Notes

Cut pieces as listed either using a rotary cutter and rotary ruler or the templates from those starting on page 87.

Refer to the General Instructions for a list of basic sewing supplies and tools needed and for instructions to finish your pot holders.

Refer to the Piecing Diagram given with each block for assembly ideas.

End of the Path

Fabric & Piece Requirements

- 1 S3 green tonal
- 2 - 1½" x 3½" each light A and dark B scraps
- 2 - 1½" x 5½" each light C and dark D scraps
- 2 - 1½" x 7½" each light E and dark F scraps
- 1 - 2" x 36" strip purple print for binding

Instructions

1. Sew pieces around S3 in alphabetical order using a partial seam at the beginning of each round referring to the General Instructions to complete the pieced block; press seams toward the most recently added strip as you sew.

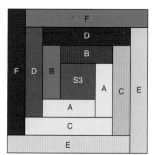

End of the Path
Placement Diagram
8" x 8"

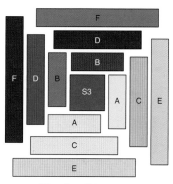

Piecing Diagram

Amazing

Fabric & Piece Requirements

- 2 S3 each 2 different green tonals
- 4 each 1½" x 3½" light A and D scraps
- 4 each 1½" x 3½" dark B and C scraps
- 1 - 2" x 36" strip purple print for binding

Instructions

1. Sew strips to S3 squares in alphabetical order using a partial seam at the beginning of each round referring to the General Instructions to complete four S3 units; press seams toward the most recently added strip as you sew.

2. Join two S3 units to make a row; press seam in one direction. Repeat to make two rows.

3. Join the rows to complete the pieced block; press seam in one direction.

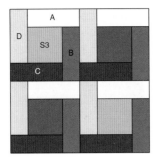

Amazing
Placement Diagram
8" x 8"

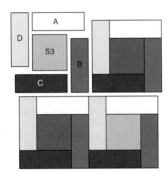

Piecing Diagram

Violet Patches

Fabric & Piece Requirements
- 4 S9 each gold and green tonals
- 28 S9 assorted colors
- 4 - 1½" x 2½" each purple print A and gold tonal B
- 4 - 1½" x 3½" C purple print
- 1 - 2" x 36" strip purple/black print for binding

Instructions
1. Join one each green and gold S9; press seam toward darker fabric.
2. Add A to the S9 unit; press seam toward A.
3. Sew B to the A-S9 unit and add C to make an A-B-C unit as shown in Figure 1; press seams toward B and then C.

Figure 1

4. Join three assorted S9 squares; press seams in one direction. Add to the C side of the A-B-C unit as shown in Figure 2; press seams toward C.

Figure 2

5. Join four assorted S9 squares; press seams in one direction. Add to the A-B-C unit, again referring to Figure 2 to complete a block quarter; press seam toward the S9 strip.
6. Repeat steps 1–5 to complete four block quarters.
7. Arrange and join the block quarters to make two rows; press seams in rows in opposite directions. Join the rows to complete the pieced block; press seam in one direction.

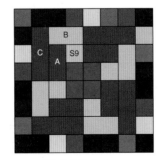

Violet Patches
Placement Diagram
8" x 8"

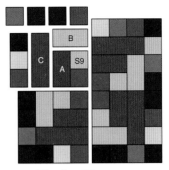

Piecing Diagram

Rose Arbor

Fabric & Piece Requirements
- 1 S3 cream print
- 8 S9 cream print
- 4 T32 green tonal
- 4 - 1½" x 2½" gold tonal B
- 8 - 1½" x 2½" maize solid A
- 1 - 2" x 36" strip rose print for binding

Instructions
1. Sew S9 to one end of each A piece; press seams toward A.
2. Sew four A-S9 units to S3 using a partial seam to complete the center unit referring to the General Instructions; press seams toward A-S9 units.
3. Sew B to the S9 end of the remaining A-S9 units; press seams toward B.

  American School of Needlework • Berne, Indiana 46711 • DRGnetwork.com

4. Sew the A-B-S9 strips to the center unit with partial seams referring to the General Instructions; press seams toward the A-B-S9 strips.

5. Sew T32 to each side of the pieced unit to complete the pieced block; press seams toward T32.

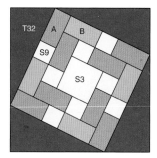

Rose Arbor
Placement Diagram
8" x 8"

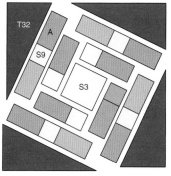

Piecing Diagram

Climbing Roses

Fabric & Piece Requirements
• 4 S3 cream print
• 2 S9 each blue solid and blue tonal
• 4 S9 cream print
• 2 - 1½" x 3½" each blue solid A and blue tonal B
• 4 - 1½" x 7½" brown print C
• 1 - 2" x 36" strip green print for binding

Instructions

1. Sew a cream S9 to a blue solid S9; press seam toward darker fabric.

2. Sew the S9 unit to S3 and add A to complete a block quarter as shown in Figure 3; press seam toward S3 and A. Repeat to make two each blue solid and blue tonal block quarters.

Figure 3

3. Join one each blue solid and blue tonal block quarters referring to the Piecing Diagram to make a row; press seam in one direction. Repeat to complete two rows; join the rows to complete the block center. Press seam in one direction.

4. Sew a C strip to each side of the block center using partial seams referring to the General Instructions to complete the pieced block.

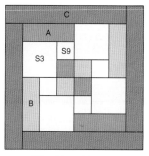

Climbing Roses
Placement Diagram
8" x 8"

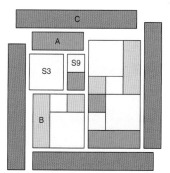

Piecing Diagram

Organic Garden

Garden paths outline the flower beds in these pot holders.

Project Notes

Cut pieces as listed either using a rotary cutter and rotary ruler or the templates from those starting on page 87.

Refer to the General Instructions for a list of basic sewing supplies and tools needed and for instructions to finish your pot holders.

Refer to the Piecing Diagram given with each block for assembly ideas.

All Natural

Fabric & Piece Requirements

• 1 S7 black print
• 4 S10 each green solid and red print
• 4 - 1¾" x 4½" A gray print
• 4 - 1¾" x 2" B red print
• 4 - 1¾" x 3½" C cream print
• 1 - 2" x 36" strip rose print for binding

Instructions

1. Sew B to one end of A; press seam toward B. Repeat to make four A-B units.
2. Join one each green and red S10 with C; press seams toward green S10. Repeat to make four C-S10 units.
3. Sew an A-B unit to a C-S10 unit to make a side unit as shown in Figure 1; press seam toward the A-B unit. Repeat to make four side units.

Figure 1

4. Sew a side unit to S7 using a partial seam referring to the General Instructions to complete the pieced block; press seams away from S7.

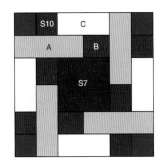

All Natural
Placement Diagram
8" x 8"

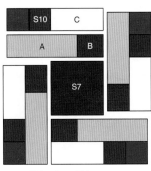

Piecing Diagram

Salad Greens

Fabric & Piece Requirements

• 1 S8 red print
• 4 S10 each cream and green tonals
• 4 T27 rose solid
• 4 M2 green tonal
• 4 M21 burgundy solid
• 4 - 1¾" x 2" A burgundy print
• 4 - 1¾" x 3½" B cream tonal
• 1 - 2" x 36" strip lavender print for binding

American School of Needlework • Berne, Indiana 46711 • DRGnetwork.com

Instructions

1. Sew a T27 to each side of S8 to complete the center unit; press seams toward T27.

2. Sew M2 to M21 and add A to the M21 end to make an A-M unit; press seams toward M21 and A.

3. Sew a cream S10 and a green S10 to one end of B; press seams toward the green S10.

4. Sew the B-S10 unit to the A-M unit to complete a side unit as shown in Figure 2; press seams toward the B-S10 unit.

5. Repeat steps 2–4 to complete four side units.

6. Sew a side unit to each side of the center unit using a partial seam referring to the General Instructions to complete the pieced block; press seams toward the side units.

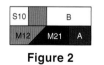

Figure 2

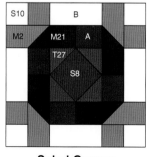

Salad Greens
Placement Diagram
8" x 8"

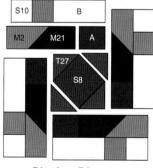

Piecing Diagram

Falling Leaves

Introduce some appliqué and embroidery to your quilted pot holders with these leaf designs.

Project Notes

Cut pieces as listed either using a rotary cutter and rotary ruler or the templates from those starting on page 87.

Refer to the General Instructions for a list of basic sewing supplies and tools needed and for instructions to finish your pot holders.

Refer to the Piecing Diagram given with each block for assembly ideas.

Green Leaf

Fabric & Piece Requirements

- 1 S11 brown solid
- Assorted coordinating scraps cut into 3"-long strips in varying widths from ½"–2" wide for A
- 4 - 1" x 5¼" B green plaid
- 4 - 1½" x 2¾" C brown solid
- Scrap green mottled for appliqué
- 1 - 2" x 36" strip burgundy print for binding
- Light green embroidery floss

Instructions

1. Referring to Figure 1, join a variety of scrap strips to make an A row; trim the A row to 2¼" x 5¼". Repeat to make four A rows.

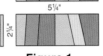

Figure 1

2. Sew B to one long side of each A row; press seam toward B. Repeat to make four A-B units.

3. Sew C to one end of each A-B unit to complete a side unit; press seams toward C.

4. Sew a side unit to each side of S11 with partial seams referring to the General Instructions to complete the pieced center; press seams toward the side units.

5. Cut, prepare and stitch leaf piece to the pieced center using pattern given on page 88 and referring to the General Instructions and the Placement Diagram.

6. Stem-stitch detail lines given with pattern using 2 strands light green embroidery floss.

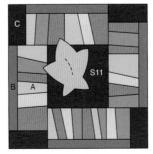

Green Leaf
Placement Diagram
8" x 8"

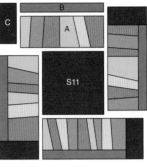

Piecing Diagram

Oak Leaf

Fabric & Piece Requirements

- 1 S11 violet print
- 4 - 2" x 2½" A violet print
- 4 - 1¼" x 4½" each gray print B and lavender solid C
- 4 - 1¼" x 6¼" D tan solid
- Scrap orange solid for leaf appliqué
- 1 - 2" x 36" strip burgundy print for binding
- Gray and rust embroidery floss

Instructions

1. Sew B to C along the length; press seam toward B. Repeat to make four B-C units.

2. Add A to one end of each B-C unit; press seams toward A.

3. Add D to each A-B-C unit; press seams toward D.

4. Sew the A-B-C-D units to S11 using a partial seam referring to the General Instructions; press seams away from S11.

5. Cut, prepare and stitch leaf piece to the pieced center using pattern given on page 88 and referring to the General Instructions and the Placement Diagram.

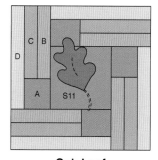

Oak Leaf
Placement Diagram
8" x 8"

6. Stem-stitch detail lines given with pattern using 2 strands light gray and rust embroidery floss.

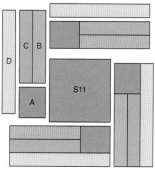

Piecing Diagram

Fall Walk

Fabric & Piece Requirements
- 1 S11 brown print
- 4 T24 each tan and brown prints
- 4 - 1¼" x 4½" each rose print A and cream tonal B
- 4 - 1¼" x 6¼" C violet print
- 1 - 2" x 36" strip cream print for binding

Instructions

1. Sew a tan T24 to a brown T24 along the diagonal; press seam toward darker fabric. Repeat to make four T24 units.

2. Sew A to B along the length; press seam toward A. Repeat to make four A-B units.

3. Add a T24 unit to one end of each A-B unit; press seams toward A-B.

4. Add C to each A-B-T24 unit to make side units; press seams toward C.

5. Sew the side units to S11 using a partial seam referring to the General Instructions; press seams away from S11.

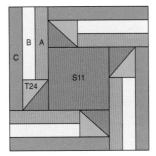

Fall Walk
Placement Diagram
8" x 8"

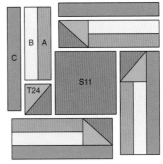

Piecing Diagram

Dramatic Impact

The addition of black fabric makes the designs in this set of theatrical-named blocks stand out.

Project Notes
Cut pieces as listed either using a rotary cutter and rotary ruler or the templates from those starting on page 87.

Refer to the General Instructions for a list of basic sewing supplies and tools needed and for instructions to finish your pot holders.

Refer to the Piecing Diagram given with each block for assembly ideas.

Gypsy Lee

Fabric & Piece Requirements
• 1 S3 floral
• 4 S3 black print
• 8 T5 white dot (reverse 4 for T5R)
• 4 T6 black floral
• 2 - 1½" x 6½" A rose tonal
• 2 - 1½" x 8½" B rose tonal
• 1 - 2" x 36" strip burgundy print for binding

Instructions
1. Sew T5 and T5R to T6 to make a side unit; press seams away from T6. Repeat to make four side units.

2. Sew a side unit to opposite sides of the floral S3 to make the center row; press seams toward S3.

3. Sew a black S3 to each side of a side unit to make a side row; press seams away from the side unit. Repeat to make two side rows.

4. Sew the center row between the side rows; press seams away from the center row.

5. Sew A to the top and bottom and B to opposite sides of the pieced center; press seams toward A and B to complete the pieced block.

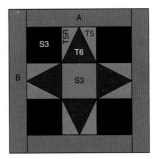

Gypsy Lee
Placement Diagram
8" x 8"

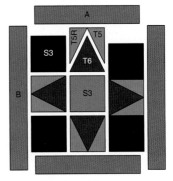

Piecing Diagram

American School of Needlework • Berne, Indiana 46711 • DRGnetwork.com

Stagestruck

Fabric & Piece Requirements
- 1 S2 majenta mottled
- 4 S3 purple tonal
- 16 T5 white solid (reverse 8 for T5R)
- 8 T6 black floral
- 4 T18 black print
- 1 - 2" x 36" strip purple print for binding

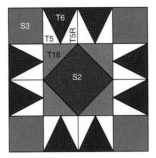

Stagestruck
Placement Diagram
8" x 8"

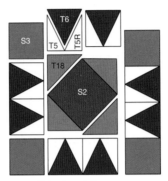

Piecing Diagram

Instructions
1. Sew T18 to each side of S2 to complete the center unit; press seams toward T18.
2. Sew T5 and T5R to T6 to complete a T unit; press seams away from T6. Repeat to make eight T units.
3. Join two T units to complete a side unit; press seam in one direction. Repeat to make four side units.
4. Sew a side unit to opposite sides of the center unit to complete the center row; press seams toward the center row.
5. Sew S3 to each end of each remaining side unit to make side rows; press seams toward S3.
6. Sew the side rows to opposite sides of the center row to complete the pieced block; press seams toward the side rows.

Bright Lights

Fabric & Piece Requirements
- 2 S3 each white solid and peach mottled
- 4 S3 black solid
- 16 T5 cream tonal (reverse 8 for T5R)
- 8 T6 black print
- 1 - 2" x 36" strip rust mottled for binding

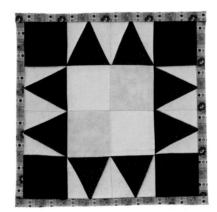

Instructions
1. Sew a white S3 to a peach S3; press seam toward darker fabric. Repeat to make two S3 rows.
2. Join the S3 rows to complete the block center; press seam in one direction.
3. Sew T5 and T5R to T6 to complete a T unit; press seams away from T6. Repeat to make eight T units.
4. Join two T units to complete a side unit; press seam in one direction. Repeat to make four side units.
5. Sew a side unit to opposite sides of the center unit to complete the center row; press seams toward the center row.
6. Sew S3 to each end of each remaining side unit to make side rows; press seams toward S3.
7. Sew the side rows to opposite sides of the center row to complete the pieced block; press seams toward the side rows.

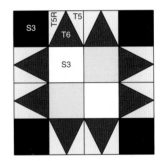

Bright Lights
Placement Diagram
8" x 8"

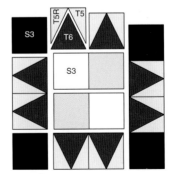

Piecing Diagram

Opening Night

Fabric & Piece Requirements
- 4 S3 black print
- 1 S4 black dot
- 4 T4 white dot
- 8 T5 black dot (reverse 4 for T5R)
- 4 T6 black dot
- 2 - 1½" x 6½" A yellow print
- 2 - 1½" x 8½" B yellow print
- 1 - 2" x 36" strip rust mottled for binding

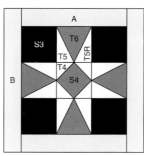

Opening Night
Placement Diagram
8" x 8"

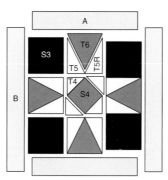

Piecing Diagram

Instructions
1. Sew T4 to each side of S4 to complete the center unit; press seams toward T4.
2. Sew T5 and T5R to T6 to complete a side unit; press seams away from T6. Repeat to make four side units.
3. Sew a side unit to opposite sides of the center unit to complete the center row; press seams toward the center row.
4. Sew S3 to opposite sides of each remaining side unit to make side rows; press seams toward S3.
5. Sew a side row to opposite sides of the center row; press seams toward side rows.
6. Sew A to the top and bottom and B to opposite sides of the pieced rows to complete the pieced block; press seams toward A and B.

Repertory Group

Fabric & Piece Requirements
- 5 S4 black dot
- 20 T4 white dot
- 8 T5 gray mottled (reverse 4 for T5R)
- 4 T6 black solid
- 6 - 1" x 2½" A gray print
- 2 - 1" x 7½" B gray print
- 2 - 1" x 7½" C cream tonal
- 2 - 1" x 8½" D cream tonal
- 1 - 2" x 36" strip black solid for binding

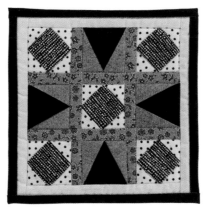

Instructions
1. Sew T4 to each side of S4 to complete an S4 unit; press seams toward T4. Repeat to make five S4 units.
2. Sew T5 and T5R to T6 to complete a T unit; press seams away from T6. Repeat to make four T units.
3. Join one T unit, two S4 units and two A strips to complete a side row; press seams toward A. Repeat to make two side rows.
4. Join one S4 unit with two T units and two A strips to complete the center row; press seams toward A.
5. Join the side and center rows with B to complete the pieced center; press seams toward B.
6. Sew C to opposite sides and D to the top and bottom of the pieced center to complete the pieced block; press seams toward C and D.

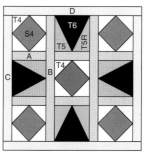

Repertory Group
Placement Diagram
8" x 8"

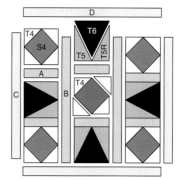

Piecing Diagram

Walk of Fame

Fabric & Piece Requirements
- 3 S4 black floral
- 12 T4 black dot
- 12 T5 white dot (reverse 6 for T5R)
- 6 T6 black dot
- 2 - 1½" x 6½" A black floral
- 2 - 1½" x 8½" B black floral
- 1 - 2" x 36" strip wine solid for binding

Instructions
1. Sew T4 to each side of S4 to complete an S4 unit; press seams toward T4. Repeat to make three S4 units.
2. Sew T5 and T5R to T6 to complete a T unit; press seams away from T6. Repeat to make 6 T units.
3. Sew a T unit to opposite sides of an S4 unit to complete one row; repeat to make three rows. Press seams of one toward the T units and two toward the S4 unit.
4. Join the rows, alternating seam pressing to complete the pieced center; press seams in one direction.
5. Sew A to opposite sides and B to the top and bottom of the pieced center to complete the pieced block; press seams toward A and B.

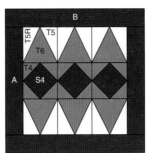

Walk of Fame
Placement Diagram
8" x 8"

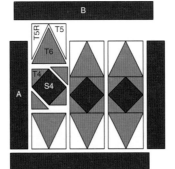

Piecing Diagram

Highs & Lows

Fabric & Piece Requirements
- 16 T5 each gray mottled and black print (reverse 8 of each for T5R)
- 8 T6 each black solid and gray print
- 1 - 2" x 36" strip pink stripe for binding

Instructions
1. Sew a black T5 and T5R to a gray print T6 to make a gray T unit; press seams away from T6. Repeat to make eight each gray and black T units.
2. Join four gray T units to make a gray row; press seams in one direction. Repeat to make two gray rows.
3. Join four black T units to make a black row; press seams in one direction. Repeat to make two black rows.
4. Arrange and join the rows referring to the Piecing Diagram to complete the pieced block; press seams in one direction.

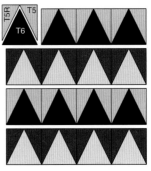

Piecing Diagram

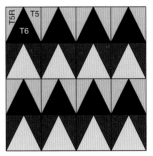

Highs & Lows
Placement Diagram
8" x 8"

   American School of Needlework • Berne, Indiana 46711 • DRGnetwork.com

American Pride

American history is reflected in the names of the block designs used to make the American Pride set of pot holders.

Project Notes

Cut pieces as listed either using a rotary cutter and rotary ruler or the templates from those starting on page 87.

Refer to the General Instructions for a list of basic sewing supplies and tools needed and for instructions to finish your pot holders.

Refer to the Piecing Diagram given with each block for assembly ideas.

Freedom Rings

Fabric & Piece Requirements

- 4 M8 light blue mottled
- 8 S9 each black print and cream/red check
- 8 T8 red tonal (reverse 4 for T8R)
- 4 - 2½" x 4½" A blue mottled
- 1 - 2" x 36" strip blue tonal for binding

Instructions

1. Sew T8 and T8R to opposite sides of M8 to make an M-T unit; press seams away from M8. Repeat to make four M-T units.
2. Join two M-T units; press seam in one direction. Repeat and press seam in the opposite direction. Join the units to complete the block center.
3. Sew A to opposite sides of the block center to make the center row; press seams toward A.

4. Sew a cream S9 to a black S9 to make an S unit; press seam toward darker fabric. Repeat to make eight S units.
5. Join two S units to make a corner unit; press seam in one direction. Repeat to make four corner units.
6. Sew a corner unit to each end of each remaining A to complete two side rows; press seams toward A.
7. Sew a side row to each side of the center row to complete the pieced block; press seams away from the center row.

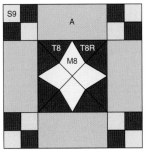

Freedom Rings
Placement Diagram
8" x 8"

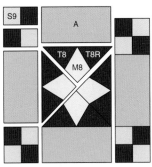

Piecing Diagram

Stars & Stripes

Fabric & Piece Requirements

- 4 M8 light blue mottled
- 8 T8 red tonal (reverse 4 for T8R)
- 2 - 1½" x 4½" each red/cream check A and navy print B
- 2 - 1½" x 8½" each red/cream check C and navy print D
- 1 - 2" x 36" strip rust mottled for binding

Instructions

1. Piece the corner unit referring to steps 1 and 2 for Freedom Rings.
2. Sew A to B to A to B; press seams toward B.
3. Sew the A-B unit to the corner unit to complete the top unit; press seam toward A-B.
4. Sew C to D to C to D to complete the bottom unit; press seams toward D.
5. Sew the bottom unit to the bottom edge of the top unit to complete the pieced block; press seam toward the bottom unit.

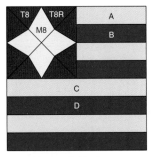

Stars & Stripes
Placement Diagram
8" x 8"

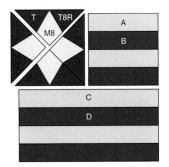

Piecing Diagram

Revolution

Fabric & Piece Requirements
- 8 M8 white/red print
- 16 T8 red print (reverse 8 for T8R)
- 4 T25 each white/navy dot and black print
- 4 - 1¼" x 5⅝" A rust solid
- 1 - 2" x 36" strip rust mottled for binding

Instructions
1. Sew a white T25 to a black T25 to make a T unit; press seam toward darker fabric. Repeat to make four T units.
2. Join two T units to make a row as shown in Figure 1; press seam toward darker fabric. Repeat to make two rows. Join the rows to complete the center unit, again referring to Figure 1; press seam in one direction.

Figure 1

3. Sew an A strip to each side of the center unit using partial seams referring to the General Instructions.
4. Sew T8 and T8R to opposite sides of M8 to make an M-T unit; press seams away from M8. Repeat to make eight M-T units.
5. Join two M-T units as shown in Figure 2 to make a corner unit; press seam in one direction. Repeat to make four corner units.

Figure 2

6. Sew a corner unit to each side of the framed center unit to complete the pieced block; press seams toward the corner units.

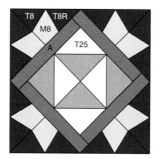

Revolution
Placement Diagram
8" x 8"

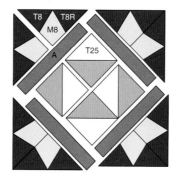

Piecing Diagram

Boston Tea Party

Fabric & Piece Requirements
- 8 M8 light blue mottled
- 2 S6 each white/red print and pink print
- 16 T8 black print (reverse 8 for T8R)
- 2 - ⅞" x 3⅛" A dark pink print
- 2 - ⅞" x 6⅛" B dark pink print
- 1 - 2" x 36" strip blue tonal for binding

Instructions
1. Sew A between a white and pink S6; press seams toward A. Repeat to make two A-S6 units.
2. Join the two A-S6 units with B to complete the center unit; press seams toward B.

3. Sew T8 and T8R to opposite sides of M8 to make an M-T unit; press seams away from M8. Repeat to make eight M-T units.
4. Join two M-T units to make a corner unit (as in Figure 2 for Revolution); press seam in one direction. Repeat to make four corner units.
5. Sew a corner unit to each side of the center unit to complete the pieced block; press seams toward the corner units.

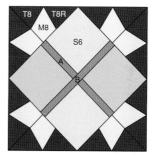

Boston Tea Party
Placement Diagram
8" x 8"

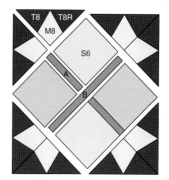

Piecing Diagram

Fascinating Twirls

Twirling designs add movement to the pot holders in this colorful collection.

Project Notes

Cut pieces as listed either using a rotary cutter and rotary ruler or the templates from those starting on page 87.

Refer to the General Instructions for a list of basic sewing supplies and tools needed and for instructions to finish your pot holders.

Refer to the Piecing Diagram given with each block for assembly ideas.

Whirling Tops

Fabric & Piece Requirements

- 16 M22 brown solid
- 16 T13 coral tonal
- 1 - 2" x 36" strip red tonal for binding

Instructions

1. Sew T13 to M22 to complete a T-M unit; press seam toward M22. Repeat to make 16 T-M units.
2. Join four T-M units to make make a block quarter; press seams in opposite directions and then in one direction. Repeat to make four block quarters.

3. Join the block quarters to make two rows; repeat and press seams in rows in opposite directions.
4. Join the rows to complete the pieced block; press seam in one direction.

Whirling Tops
Placement Diagram
8" x 8"

Piecing Diagram

Pirouettes

Fabric & Piece Requirements

- 8 M27 lavender solid
- 4 S3 each pink and coral tonals
- 8 T13 coral tonal
- 8 T31 fuchsia solid
- 1 - 2" x 36" strip blue print for binding

Instructions

1. Sew T13 and T31 to M27 to make an M-T unit; press seams away from M27. Repeat to make eight units.
2. Join two M-T units to make a row; press seam in one direction. Repeat to make two rows. Join the rows to complete an M-T block quarter; press seam in one direction. Repeat to make two M-T block quarters.
3. Sew a pink S3 to a fuchsia S3 to make an S unit; press seam toward darker fabric. Repeat to make four S units.
4. Join two S units to make an S block quarter; press seam in one direction. Repeat to make two S block quarters.
5. Join one each M-T and S block quarter to make a row; press seam toward S block quarter. Repeat to make two rows. Join the rows to complete the pieced block; press seam in one direction.

   American School of Needlework · Berne, Indiana 46711 · DRGnetwork.com

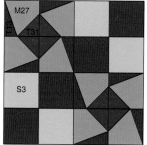

Pirouettes
Placement Diagram
8" x 8"

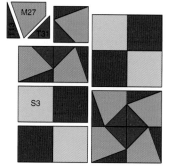

Piecing Diagram

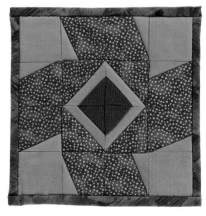

Eye of the Storm

Fabric & Piece Requirements
- 8 M22 coral tonal
- 4 S3 lavender solid
- 8 T13 lavender solid
- 4 T18 coral tonal
- 4 T27 brown solid
- 4 - ⅞" x 4" A lavender solid
- 1 - 2" x 36" strip blue print for binding

Instructions
1. Sew A to T27; press seam toward T27. Trim A even with edges of T27 as shown in Figure 1. Repeat to make four A-T27 units.

Figure 1

2. Sew T18 to an A-T27 unit to make an A-T unit; press seam away from A. Repeat to make four A-T units.

3. Sew T13 to M22 to make an M-T unit; press seam toward M22. Repeat to make eight M-T units.

4. To make one block quarter, sew one M-T unit to one A-T unit; press seam toward the A-T unit.

5. Sew S3 to an M-T unit; press seam toward S3.

6. Join the units pieced in steps 4 and 5 to complete a block quarter; press seam in one direction. Repeat to make four block quarters.

7. Join two block quarters to make a row; press seam in one direction. Repeat to make two rows. Join the rows to complete the pieced block; press seam in one direction.

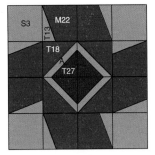

Eye of the Storm
Placement Diagram
8" x 8"

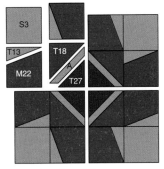

Piecing Diagram

Down-Home Fun

Crazy patchwork pieces add a nostalgic feeling to the pot holders in this collection.

Project Notes

Refer to the General Instructions to complete crazy patchwork from which to cut pieces for the pot holders in this collection.

Cut pieces as listed either using a rotary cutter and rotary ruler or the templates from those starting on page 87.

Refer to the General Instructions for a list of basic sewing supplies and tools needed and for instructions to finish your pot holders.

Refer to the Piecing Diagram given with each block for assembly ideas.

Great-Grandma

Fabric & Piece Requirements
• 2 S1 cream/red print
• 2 - 4½" x 4½" A crazy-patchwork
• 1 - 2" x 36" strip black floral for binding

Instructions

1. Sew S1 to A to make a row; press seam toward S1. Repeat to make two rows.

2. Join the rows to complete the pieced block; press seam in one direction.

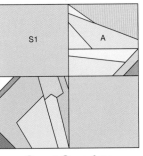

Great-Grandma
Placement Diagram
8" x 8"

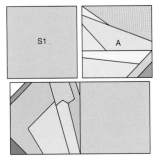

Piecing Diagram

Apron Strings

Fabric & Piece Requirements
- 3 - 2½" x 8½" A crazy-patchwork
- 2 - 1½" x 8½" B black check
- 1 - 2" x 36" strip pink stripe
  for binding

Instructions
1. Join the three crazy-patchwork A strips with B to complete the pieced top; press seams toward B.

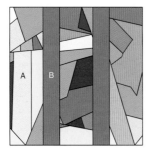

Apron Strings
Placement Diagram
8" x 8"

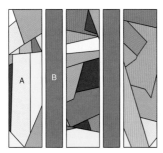

Piecing Diagram

Warm Heart

Fabric & Piece Requirements
- 1 M32 crazy-patchwork
- 4 T28 cream/red print (reverse 2 for T28R)
- 2 - 1½" x 8½" A rose print
- 1 - 2" x 36" strip gold tonal for binding

Instructions
1. Sew T28R pieces to opposite sides of M32 as shown in Figure 1; press seam toward T28R. Trim the ends of the T28R pieces even with the edges of M32, again referring to Figure 1.

Figure 1

2. Sew T28 to the remaining sides of M32; press seams toward T28.
3. Sew A to opposite long sides of the pieced center to complete the pieced block; press seams toward A.

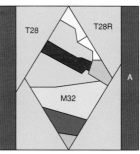

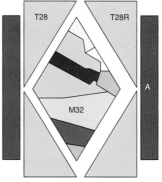

Warm Heart
Placement Diagram
8" x 8"

Piecing Diagram

Across the Table

Fabric & Piece Requirements
- 2 M7 crazy-patchwork
- 2 M38 crazy-patchwork
- 4 T30 orange tonal (reverse 2 for T30R)
- 2 - 1¼" x 4" A red print
- 1 - 1¼" x 7½" B red print
- 1 - 2" x 36" strip black floral for binding

Instructions

1. Center and sew A between one each M7 and M38 pieces as shown in Figure 2; press seams toward A. Trim A ends even with edges of the M pieces, again referring to Figure 2. Repeat to make two A-M units.

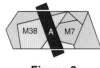

Figure 2

2. Center and sew B between two A-M units as shown in Figure 3; press seams toward B. Trim B ends even with edges of the two joined units to complete the center unit, again referring to Figure 3.

Figure 3

3. Sew T30R to opposite sides of the center unit referring to Figure 4, press seams toward T30R. Trim excess at ends even with the center unit, again referring to Figure 4.

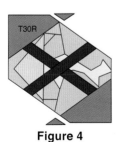

Figure 4

4. Add T30 pieces to the remaining sides of the center unit to complete the pieced block; press seams toward T30.

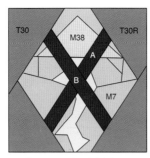

Across the Table
Placement Diagram
8" x 8"

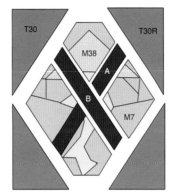

Piecing Diagram

Backyard Gossip

Fabric & Piece Requirements
- 2 M10 red print
- 2 T10 crazy-patchwork
- 2 - 1½" x 8½" pink print A
- 1 - 2" x 36" strip black floral for binding

Instructions

1. Sew a T10 to M10; press seam toward M10. Repeat to make two T-M units.

2. Join the T-M units to complete the pieced center; press seam in one direction.

3. Sew A to opposite long sides to complete the pieced block; press seams toward A.

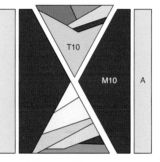

Backyard Gossip
Placement Diagram
8" x 8"

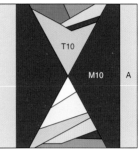

Piecing Diagram

Spinovation

The spinning centers of these pot holders seem to be in perpetual motion.

Project Notes

Cut pieces as listed either using a rotary cutter and rotary ruler or the templates from those starting on page 87.

Refer to the General Instructions for a list of basic sewing supplies and tools needed and for instructions to finish your pot holders.

Refer to the Piecing Diagram given with each block for assembly ideas.

Spin Art

Fabric & Piece Requirements

• 4 M33 light green print
• 4 T18 olive print
• 4 T19 olive print
• 4 - 1½" x 3½" A light green print
• 4 - 1½" x 7½" B yellow dot
• 1 - 2" x 36" strip brown print for binding

1. Sew M33 to T19 and add T18 to make an M-T unit; press seam toward T19 and then T18. Repeat to make four M-T units.

2. Sew A to each M-T unit to make a quarter-unit; press seams toward A.

3. Join two quarter-units to make a row; press seam in one direction. Repeat to make two rows.

4. Join the rows to complete the block center; press seam in one direction.

5. Sew B to each side of the block center using a partial seam referring to the General Instructions to complete the pieced block; press seams toward B.

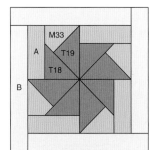

Spin Art
Placement Diagram
8" x 8"

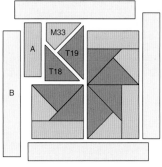

Piecing Diagram

Pinwheel

Fabric & Piece Requirements

• 4 M33 olive print
• 4 T18 blue mottled
• 4 T19 light green print
• 4 - 1½" x 3½" A light blue tonal
• 4 - 1½" x 7½" B yellow dot
• 1 - 2" x 36" strip blue floral for binding

Instructions

1. Refer to all steps for piecing Spin Art. **Note:** *The blocks use the same pieces and units, but they are stitched together in a different layout. Refer to the Piecing Diagram for positioning of units for stitching.*

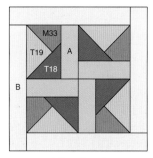

Pinwheel
Placement Diagram
8" x 8"

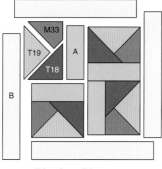

Piecing Diagram

Carousel

Fabric & Piece Requirements
- 4 M11 light blue tonal
- 4 M30 navy print
- 4 M33 navy solid
- 1 S9 blue mottled
- 4 T1 navy print
- 4 T18 light green tonal
- 4 T19 blue mottled
- 4 T21 light green solid
- 1 - 2" x 36" strip light green mottled for binding

Instructions
1. Sew M33 to T19 and add T18 to make an M-T unit; press seam toward T19 and then T18. Repeat to make four M-T units.

2. Sew the M-T units around S using a partial seam referring to the General Instructions to complete the block center; press seams toward the M-T units.

3. Sew M11 between T1 and M30 to make a side unit; press seams away from T1. Repeat to make four side units.

4. Sew a side unit to each side of the block center; press seams toward the side units.

5. Sew T21 to each long side of the pieced unit to complete the pieced block; press seams toward T21.

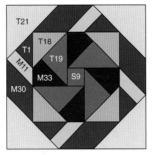

Carousel
Placement Diagram
8" x 8"

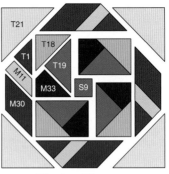

Piecing Diagram

Fresh Fruit

Appliquéd fruit make these pot holders an appetizing addition to anyone's kitchen.

Project Notes
Cut pieces as listed either using a rotary cutter and rotary ruler or the templates from those starting on page 87.

Refer to the General Instructions for a list of basic sewing supplies and tools needed and for instructions to finish your pot holders.

Refer to the Piecing Diagram given with each block for assembly ideas.

Orange Delight

Fabric & Piece Requirements
• 4 T18 white/purple print
• 1 - 5½" x 5½" A light orange print
• 4 - 1" x 6" B orange print
• 4 - 1½" x 6¾" C strips light blue mottled
• Scraps orange and green solids and green mottled for appliqué
• 1 - 2" x 36" strip orange print for binding
• Gold and green embroidery floss

Instructions
1. Using the wrong side of A as the right side, sew B to each side of A using a partial seam referring to the General Instructions; press seams toward B.

2. Trim each end of each C strip at a 45-degree angle as shown in Figure 1.

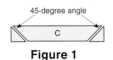

45-degree angle

C

Figure 1

3. Center and sew C to each side of the A-B unit; press seams toward C.

4. Sew T18 to each corner to complete the pieced block.

5. Cut, prepare and appliqué the orange motif to the pieced block using patterns given on page 88 and referring to the General Instructions.

6. Add X marks on the orange shape using 2 strands gold embroidery floss.

7. Stem-stitch the orange stem using 2 strands green embroidery floss to complete the block.

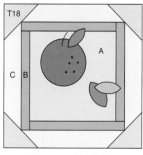

Orange Delight
Placement Diagram
8" x 8"

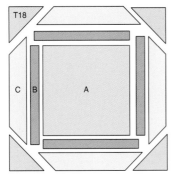

Piecing Diagram

Cherry Trio

Fabric & Piece Requirements
- 4 T18 yellow print
- 1 - 5½" x 5½" A yellow dot
- 2 - 1" x 5½" B white/purple print
- 2 - 1" x 6½" C white/purple print
- 4 - 1½" x 6¾" D strips light blue mottled
- Scraps red and green solids for appliqué
- 1 - 2" x 36" strip peach print for binding
- Pink and green embroidery floss

Instructions
1. Sew B to opposite sides and C to the top and bottom of A; press seams toward B and C.
2. Trim each end of each D strip at a 45-degree angle as for Orange Delight.
3. Center and sew D to each side of the A-B-C unit; press seams toward D.
4. Sew T18 to each corner to complete the pieced block.
5. Cut, prepare and appliqué the cherry motif to the pieced block using patterns given on page 96 and referring to the General Instructions.
6. Satin-stitch detail lines on the cherry shapes using 2 strands pink embroidery floss.
7. Satin-stitch the leaf stems and straight-stitch leaf veins using 2 strands green embroidery floss to complete the block.

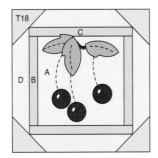

Cherry Trio
Placement Diagram
8" x 8"

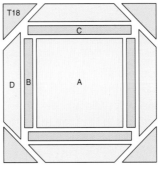

Piecing Diagram

Apple of Your Eye

Fabric & Piece Requirements
- 1 S7 blue solid
- 4 S9 gold solid
- 4 T18 white/purple print
- 4 - 1½" x 3½" A tan dot
- 2 - 1" x 5½" B gold check
- 2 - 1" x 6½" C gold check
- 4 - 1½" x 6¾" D cream solid
- Scrap rust print for appliqué
- 1 - 2" x 36" strip white/purple print for binding
- Light and dark green and gold embroidery floss

Instructions
1. Sew A to opposite sides of S7; press seams toward A.
2. Sew S9 to each end of each remaining A; press seams toward A.
3. Sew the A-S9 units to the remaining sides of the A-S7 unit to complete the block center; press seams toward the A-S9 units.

4. Sew B to the top and bottom and C to opposite sides of the block center; press seams toward B and C.

5. Trim each end of each D strip at a 45-degree angle as for Orange Delight.

6. Center and sew D to each side of the block center; press seams toward D.

7. Sew T18 to each corner to complete the pieced block.

8. Cut, prepare and appliqué the apple motif to the pieced block using patterns given on page 91 and referring to the General Instructions.

9. Satin-stitch detail lines on the apple shape using 2 strands gold embroidery floss.

10. Stem-stitch the entire leaf and leaf stem using 2 strands light and dark green embroidery floss to complete the block.

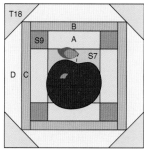

Apple of Your Eye
Placement Diagram
8" x 8"

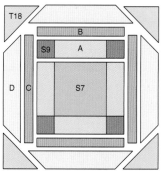

Piecing Diagram

Pear Duo

Fabric & Piece Requirements
- 1 S7 light blue solid
- 4 S9 gold print
- 4 T18 white/purple print
- 4 - 1½" x 3½" A tan dot
- 2 - 1" x 5½" B light blue mottled
- 2 - 1" x 6½" C light blue mottled
- 4 - 1½" x 6¾" D yellow dot
- Scraps gold solid and green print for appliqué
- 1 - 2" x 36" strip white/purple print for binding
- Green embroidery floss

Instructions
1. Complete the block as for Apple of Your Eye block except appliqué two pear motifs to the completed block and add an X on the pear using 2 strands green embroidery floss using patterns given on page 88 and referring to the General Instructions.

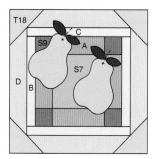

Pear Duo
Placement Diagram
8" x 8"

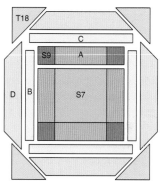

Piecing Diagram

Butterfly Beauties

Pieced butterflies are the focus of these delightful summertime pot holders.

Project Notes

Cut pieces as listed either using a rotary cutter and rotary ruler or the templates from those starting on page 87.

Refer to the General Instructions for a list of basic sewing supplies and tools needed and for instructions to finish your pot holders.

Refer to the Piecing Diagram given with each block for assembly ideas.

Blue Butterfly

Fabric & Piece Requirements

- 2 M9 aqua print (reverse 1 for M9R)
- 2 S10 each blue tonal and cream solid
- 4 T4 cream solid
- 2 T31 each aqua print and blue tonal
- 6 T31 cream solid
- 1 - 1" x 3¾" A purple tonal
- 1 - 1" x 1¾" B cream solid
- 1 - 1" x 1½" C cream solid
- 4 - 1¾" x 7¼" D yellow dot
- 1 - 2" x 36" strip cream floral for binding
- Purple and burgundy embroidery floss

Instructions

1. Sew T4 to the two short angled sides and T31 to the longer angled side of M9 to complete a wing unit; press seams away from M9. Repeat to make a reverse wing unit.

2. Sew a cream S10 to a blue S10 to make an S10 unit; press seam toward the darker fabric. Repeat to make two S10 units.

3. Sew an S10 unit to the bottom of each wing unit; press seam toward the S10 unit.

4. Sew a cream T31 to a blue T31; press seam toward darker fabric. Repeat to make two blue/cream and two aqua/cream T31 units.

5. Join one each blue/cream and aqua/cream T31 unit to make a triangle unit as shown in Figure 1; press seam toward darker unit. Repeat to make two triangle units.

Figure 1

6. Sew a triangle unit to the bottom of each wing unit to complete two side wing units; press seams toward the S10 units.

7. Sew B and C to A; press seams toward A.

8. Join the two side wing units with the A-B-C unit to complete the pieced butterfly; press seams toward the A-B-C unit.

9. Sew D to each side of the pieced butterfly using partial seams referring to the General Instructions; press seams toward D.

10. Using 2 strands purple floss, stem-stitch the butterfly antennae. Using 2 strands burgundy floss, stem-stitch wing curls to complete the pieced block.

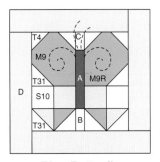

Blue Butterfly
Placement Diagram
8" x 8"

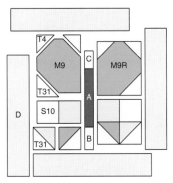

Piecing Diagram

 American School of Needlework • Berne, Indiana 46711 • DRGnetwork.com

Monarch Butterfly

Fabric & Piece Requirements
- 2 M9 orange tonal (reverse 1 for M9R)
- 2 S10 pink tonal
- 4 T4 cream solid
- 4 T31 orange tonal
- 6 T31 cream solid
- 1 - 1" x 3¾" A purple print
- 1 - 1" x 1¾" B cream solid
- 1 -1" x 1½" C cream solid
- 4 - 1¾" x 7¼" D blue print
- 1 - 2" x 36" strip purple floral for binding
- Blue and green embroidery floss

Instructions
1. Complete wing units and A-B-C unit as for Blue Butterfly.
2. Sew a cream T31 to an orange T31 to make a T31 unit; press seam toward darker fabric. Repeat to make four T31 units.
3. Sew a T31 unit to each S10 square to make two each pink and cream S10 units; press seams toward S10 squares.
4. Join one each pink and cream S10 unit to make a lower wing unit; press seam toward the pink S10 unit. Repeat to make two lower wing units.
5. Sew a lower wing unit to each wing unit to complete two side wing units.
6. Complete the pieced block referring to steps 8–10 for the Blue Butterfly using green floss for the antennae and blue floss for the wing curls.

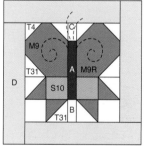

Monarch Butterfly
Placement Diagram
8" x 8"

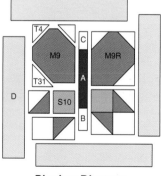

Piecing Diagram

Sweetheart Butterfly

Fabric & Piece Requirements
- 2 M9 pink tonal (reverse 1 for M9R)
- 4 S10 cream solid
- 4 T4 cream solid
- 4 T31 each lavender tonal and cream solid
- 2 T31 pink tonal
- 1 - 1" x 3¾" A wine print
- 1 - 1" x 1¾" B cream solid
- 1 -1" x 1½" C cream solid
- 4 - 1¾" x 7¼" D medium green solid
- 1 - 2" x 36" strip wine floral for binding
- Green and pink embroidery floss

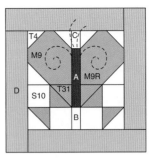

Sweetheart Butterfly
Placement Diagram
8" x 8"

Instructions
1. Piece as for Monarch Butterfly except join T31 triangles to make two each pink/lavender and cream/lavender T31 units. Refer to the Piecing Diagram for placement of the pieced units to complete the pieced block.

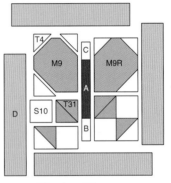

Piecing Diagram

Spring Florals

Appliquéd flowers in pastel colors hail the arrival of spring.

Project Notes
Cut pieces as listed either using a rotary cutter and rotary ruler or the templates from those starting on page 87.

Refer to the General Instructions for a list of basic sewing supplies and tools needed and for instructions to finish your pot holders.

Refer to the Piecing Diagram given with each block for assembly ideas.

Pollination

Fabric & Piece Requirements
- 2 T29 each blue mottled and lavender tonal
- 4 - 2¾" x 3½" A cream tonal
- 4 - 2¼" x 2¾" B green tonal
- 4 - 1" x 7½" C aqua check
- Scraps lavender solid and pink tonal for appliqué
- 1 - 2" x 36" strip yellow print for binding
- Pink, green and blue embroidery floss

Instructions

1. Sew a blue T29 to a lavender T29; press seam toward darker fabric. Repeat to make two T29 units.

2. Join the T29 units to complete the block center; press seam in one direction.

3. Sew B to one end of A to make a side unit; press seam toward B. Repeat to make four side units.

4. Sew a side unit to each side of the center unit using a partial seam referring to the General Instructions; press seams toward the side units.

5. Sew a C strip to each side of the pieced center using a partial seam referring to the General Instructions; press seams toward C.

6. Cut, prepare and appliqué the flower and butterfly motifs given on page 88 to the pieced block referring to the General Instructions.

7. Stem-stitch flower stems using 2 strands green embroidery floss.

8. Stem-stitch the butterfly body and antennae using 2 strands blue embroidery floss.

9. Buttonhole-stitch around the flowers using 2 strands pink embroidery floss to complete the block.

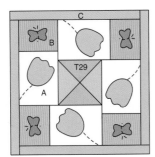

Pollination
Placement Diagram
8" x 8"

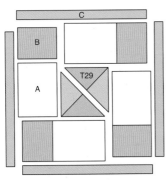

Piecing Diagram

Pretty Posies

Fabric & Piece Requirements
• 4 S5 cream solid
• 1 S7 lavender solid
• 4 S13 orange solid
• 4 - 3" x 3½" A aqua solid
• 4 - 1¼" x 2¼" each pink tonal B and orange print C
• Scraps cream and green tonals and yellow dot for appliqué
• 1 - 2" x 36" strip tan tonal for binding
• Pink and green embroidery floss

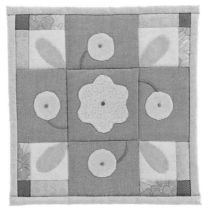

Instructions

1. Sew B to one side of S5; press seam toward B. Repeat to make four B-S5 units.

2. Sew S13 to one end of C; press seam toward C; repeat to make four C-S13 units.

3. Sew a B-S5 unit to a C-S13 unit to complete a corner unit; press seams toward the C-S13 unit. Repeat to make four corner units.

4. Sew A to opposite sides of S7 to complete the center row; press seams toward A.

5. Sew A between two corner units to complete a side row; press seams toward A. Repeat to make two side rows.

6. Sew the side rows to opposite sides of the center row to complete the block piecing; press seams toward the center row.

7. Cut, prepare and appliqué the flower and leaf motifs given on page 87 to the pieced block referring to the General Instructions.

8. Stem-stitch flower stems using 2 strands green embroidery floss.

9. Satin-stitch small flower center using 2 strands green embroidery floss and the larger flower center using 2 strands blue embroidery floss to complete the block.

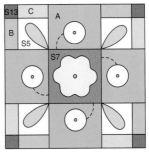

Pretty Posies
Placement Diagram
8" x 8"

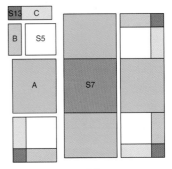

Piecing Diagram

Pot of Tulips

Fabric & Piece Requirements
• 1 - 5¼" x 6½" A light gold tonal
• 2 - 1¼" x 1½" C light gold tonal
• 2 - 2⅛" x 2¾" E light gold tonal
• 1 - 1¼" x 4½" B purple check
• 1 - 2¾" x 3¼" D purple check
• 1 - 1¼" x 6½" F lavender print
• 1 - 1" x 6½" G purple print
• 1 - 2" x 9½" H lavender solid
• Scraps lavender and pink tonals and pink and green solids for appliqué
• 1 - 2" x 40" strip light blue print for binding
• 10" pink/white flowered lace trim
• Blue and green embroidery floss

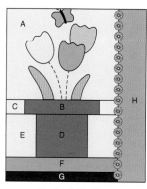

Pot of Tulips
Placement Diagram
7½" x 9"

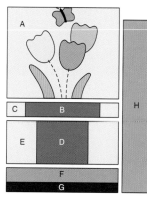

Piecing Diagram

Instructions

1. Cut, prepare and appliqué the flower and leaf motifs given on page 96 to A referring to the General Instructions.

2. Stem-stitch the flower stems using 2 strands green embroidery floss. Satin-stitch the butterfly body and antennae using 2 strands blue embroidery floss.

3. Sew C to each short end of B; press seams toward B.

4. Sew the B-C unit to A; press seam toward A.

5. Sew E to opposite sides of D; press seams toward E.

6. Sew the D-E unit to the A-B-C unit to complete the flower section; press seams toward the D-E unit.

7. Sew F and G to the bottom of the flower section and add H to the side edge referring to the Piecing Diagram for positioning; press seams toward F, G and H.

8. Center and stitch the lace trim over the seam between the pieced section and H to complete the block.

Pot of Blooms

Fabric & Piece Requirements
• 1 - 5¼" x 6½" A peach mottled
• 2 - 1¼" x 1½" C peach mottled
• 2 - 2⅛" x 2¾" E peach mottled
• 1 - 1¼" x 4½" B green tonal
• 1 - 2¾" x 3¼" D green tonal
• 1 - 1¼" x 6½" F gray print
• 1 - 1" x 6½" G aqua tonal
• 1 - 2" x 9½" H green print
• Scraps lavender and blue tonals and green mottled for appliqué
• 1 - 2" x 40" strip green tonal for binding
• 10" blue/white flowered lace trim
• Green, purple and yellow embroidery floss

Instructions

1. Complete the block as for Pot of Tulips using the appliqué motifs on page 96, except satin-stitch large flower center with 2 strands purple embroidery floss and small flower centers using 2 strands yellow embroidery floss.

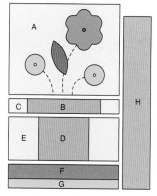

Pot of Blooms
Placement Diagram
7½" x 9"

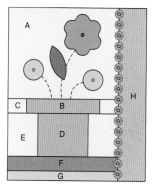

Piecing Diagram

French Countryside

Pieced flowers are fun to stitch in colors of the French countryside.

Project Notes

Cut pieces as listed either using a rotary cutter and rotary ruler or the templates from those starting on page 87.

Refer to the General Instructions for a list of basic sewing supplies and tools needed and for instructions to finish your pot holders.

Refer to the Piecing Diagram given with each block for assembly ideas.

Provençal

Fabric & Piece Requirements

- 2 M1 lavender solid (reverse 1 for M1R)
- 3 M6 lavender print
- 3 M20 gold check
- 3 M19 gold check
- 6 T4 lavender solid
- 6 T7 cream check
- 3 T23 green solid
- 2 T27 green solid
- 1 - 5¼" x 5¼" A lavender solid
- 2 - 1¼" x 3" B lavender solid
- 1 - 1¼" x 7¾" C lavender print
- 1 - 1¼" x 8½" D lavender print
- 1 - 2" x 36" strip green print for binding
- Green and purple embroidery floss

Instructions

1. To make one flower unit, sew M6 to M19 to make an M unit; press seam toward M6.

2. Sew T4 to T7; press seam toward T4. Repeat to make two T units.

3. Sew a T unit to the M unit as shown in Figure 1; press seam toward the M unit.

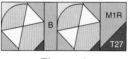

Figure 1

4. Sew the remaining T unit to M20; press seam toward M20. Sew this unit to the T-M unit as shown in Figure 2; press seam in one direction.

Figure 2

5. Add T23 to the M20 corner to complete one flower unit, again referring to Figure 2; press seam toward T23. Repeat to make three flower units.

6. Sew T27 to M1 and M1R to make one end unit and one reversed end unit; press seams toward T27.

7. Sew the end unit to the T23 side and B to the M6 side of one flower unit to complete the top unit as shown in Figure 3; press seams away from the flower unit.

Figure 3

8. Sew the top unit to A to complete the A unit; press seam toward A.

9. Join two flower units with B and add the reversed end unit to complete the side unit as shown in Figure 4; press seams away from the flower units.

Figure 4

10. Sew the side unit to the A unit referring to the Piecing Diagram; press seam toward the A unit.

11. Sew C to the bottom and D to the A side of the pieced section; press seams toward C and D.

12. Add stem lines to A using 6 strands green embroidery floss.

13. Stem-stitch flower details using 1 strand of purple embroidery floss, adding French knots at the end of each stitch line using 2 strands of purple embroidery floss to complete the block.

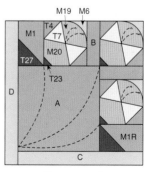

Provençal
Placement Diagram
8" x 8"

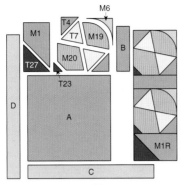

Piecing Diagram

Belle Fleurs

Fabric & Piece Requirements
- 4 M6 lavender print
- 4 M20 gold check
- 4 M19 gold check
- 8 T4 lavender solid
- 8 T7 cream check
- 4 T23 green solid
- 2 - 1¼" x 3" A lavender print
- 1 - 1¼" x 6¼" B lavender print
- 1 - 1¾" x 7½" C lavender print
- 1 - 1½" x 7½" D lavender print
- 1 - 1½" x 7¼" E lavender print
- 1 - 1¾" x 7¼" F lavender print
- 1 - 2" x 36" strip green print for binding
- Rust and green embroidery floss

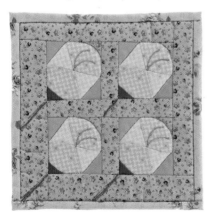

Instructions
1. Complete four flower units referring to steps 1–5 for Provençal.
2. Join two flower units with A to make a row; press seams toward A. Repeat to make two rows.
3. Join the rows with B to complete the pieced center; press seams toward B.
4. Sew C, D, E and F strips to the pieced center in alphabetical order using a partial seam referring to the General Instructions to complete the pieced block.
5. Stem-stitch flower detail lines and add French knots using 2 strands rust embroidery floss. Stem-stitch flower stems on the B, C and F pieces using 2 strands green embroidery floss referring to the block drawing for positioning.

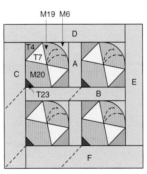

Belle Fleurs
Placement Diagram
8" x 8"

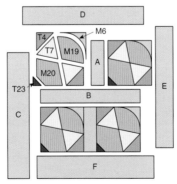

Piecing Diagram

Nosegay

Fabric & Piece Requirements
- 2 M1 peach mottled (reverse 1 for M1R)
- 3 S9 aqua print
- 12 S13 aqua print
- 2 T27 green solid
- 1 - 5¼" x 5¼" A peach mottled
- 12 - 1¼" x 1½" B blue tonal
- 2 - 1¼" x 3" C peach mottled
- 1 - 1¼" x 7¾" D lavender print
- 1 - 1¼" x 8½" E lavender print
- 1 - 2" x 36" strip light green print for binding
- Yellow, red and green embroidery floss

Instructions
1. Sew S13 to opposite sides of B to make a B row; press seams toward B. Repeat to make six B rows.
2. Sew B to opposite sides of S9 to make an S row; press seams toward F. Repeat to make three S rows.
3. Sew an S row between two B rows to complete a flower unit; press seams toward B rows. Repeat to make three flower units.
4. Sew T27 to M1 and M1R to make an end unit and a reversed end unit; press seams toward T27.

5. Sew a flower unit between C and the end unit to make a side unit as shown in Figure 5; press seams away from the flower unit.

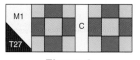

Figure 5

6. Sew a side unit to A to complete the A unit; press seam toward A.

7. Join two flower units with C and the reversed end unit to make a top unit as shown in Figure 6; press seams toward C and the reversed end unit.

Figure 6

8. Sew the top unit to the A unit; press seam toward the A unit.

9. Sew D to the bottom and E to the remaining A side of the pieced unit to complete the block piecing.

10. Add stem lines to A using 6 strands green embroidery floss.

11. Satin-stitch flower centers using 2 strands yellow embroidery floss. Straight-stitch around centers using 2 strands red embroidery floss.

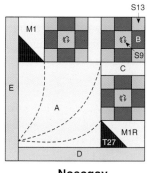

Nosegay
Placement Diagram
8" x 8"

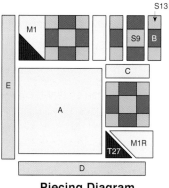
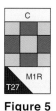

Piecing Diagram

Bouquet

Fabric & Piece Requirements
- 4 S9 white solid
- 16 S13 white solid
- 16 - 1¼" x 1½" B aqua check
- 2 - 1¼" x 3" A green tonal
- 1 - 1¼" x 6¼" C green tonal
- 1 - 1½" x 7½" D green tonal
- 1 - 1¾" x 7¼" E green tonal
- 1 - 1½" x 7¼" F green tonal
- 1 - 1¾" x 7½" G green tonal
- 1 - 2" x 36" strip light green print print for binding
- Yellow and aqua embroidery floss

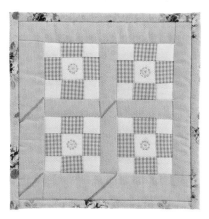

Instructions
1. Complete four flower units referring to steps 1–3 for Nosegay.

2. Join two flower units with A to make a row; press seams toward A. Repeat to make two rows.

3. Join the rows with C to complete the pieced center; press seams toward C.

4. Sew D, E, F and G strips to the pieced center in alphabetical order using a partial seam referring to the General Instructions to complete the pieced block.

5. Satin-stitch flower centers using 2 strands yellow embroidery floss. Straight-stitch around centers using 2 strands aqua embroidery floss.

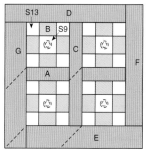

Bouquet
Placement Diagram
8" x 8"

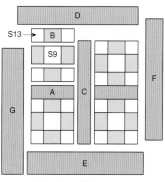

Piecing Diagram

Fruit Baskets

Pretty pieced baskets filled with appliquéd fruits should fit right into your kitchen's decor.

Project Notes

Cut pieces as listed either using a rotary cutter and rotary ruler or the templates from those starting on page 87.

Refer to the General Instructions for a list of basic sewing supplies and tools needed and for instructions to finish your pot holders.

Refer to the Piecing Diagram given with each block for assembly ideas.

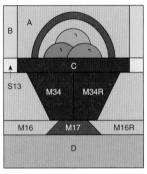

Basket of Plums
Placement Diagram
7½" x 8½"

Basket of Plums

Fabric & Piece Requirements

- 2 M16 light green tonal (reverse 1 for M16R)
- 1 M17 brown solid
- 2 M34 each burgundy print and light green tonal (reverse 1 each fabric for M34R)
- 2 S13 tan tonal
- 1 - 3¼" x 6½" A light green tonal
- 2 - 1¼" x 3¼" B light green print
- 1 - 1¼" x 6½" C burgundy print
- 1 - 2¼" x 8" D tan floral
- Scraps rust, brown and lavender solids and purple check for appliqué
- 1 - 2" x 36" strip green print for binding
- Green embroidery floss

Instructions

1. Cut, prepare and stitch appliqué pieces to A using patterns given on page 87 and referring to the General Instructions and the block drawing.

2. Sew B to each end of A to complete the A unit; press seams toward B.

3. Sew S13 to each end of C; press seam toward C.

4. Sew the C-S13 unit to the bottom edge of the A unit to complete the basket-top unit; press seams toward C-S13.

5. Sew a green M34 to a burgundy M34; press seam toward darker fabric. Repeat with the M34R pieces. Join the two units referring to the Piecing Diagram to complete the M34 unit; press seam in one direction.

6. Sew M17 between M16 and M16R to make an M unit; press seams toward M17.

7. Sew the M unit to the bottom of the M34 unit; press seams toward the M unit. Sew D to the M17 side to complete the basket-bottom unit; press seam toward D.

8. Join the basket-top and -bottom units to complete the pieced block; press seam toward the basket-top unit.

9. Stem-stitch detail lines on fruit using 2 strands green embroidery floss to finish.

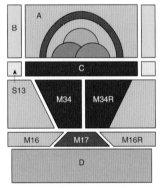

Piecing Diagram

Apple a Day

Fabric & Piece Requirements

- 2 M34 each light gold tonal and brown print (reverse 1 each fabric for M34R)
- 2 S13 each light green and brown print
- 1 - 3¼" x 6½" A light gold tonal
- 2 - 1¼" x 3¼" B gold print
- 1 - 1¼" x 6½" C brown print
- 1 - 1¼" x 2" D light green print
- 2 - 1¼" x 2¾" E light gold tonal
- 1 - 2¼" x 8" F rust plaid

American School of Needlework • Berne, Indiana 46711 • DRGnetwork.com

Instructions

1. Refer to steps 1–5 for Basket of Plums to complete the basket-top unit and M34 unit. ***Note: appliqué pattern is on page 96.***

2. Sew a brown print S13 to each short side of D; press seams toward S13. Add E to each S13 end to complete the basket-foot unit; press seams toward S13.

3. Sew F to the basket-foot unit and sew to the M34 unit to complete the basket bottom; press seam toward F.

4. Join the basket-top and -bottom units to complete the pieced block; press seam toward the basket-top unit.

5. Stem-stitch detail lines on fruit using 2 strands cream and leaf stem using 2 strands green embroidery floss to finish.

- Scraps coral and light green tonals and brown print for appliqué
- 1 - 2" x 36" strip black floral for binding
- Cream and green embroidery floss

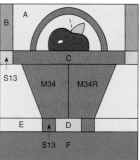

Apple a Day
Placement Diagram
7½" x 8½"

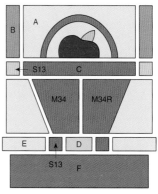

Piecing Diagram

Make Mine Diamonds

Diamond shapes stand out when stitched in bright orange against a lighter background.

Project Notes

Cut pieces as listed either using a rotary cutter and rotary ruler or the templates from those starting on page 87.

Refer to the General Instructions for a list of basic sewing supplies and tools needed and for instructions to finish your pot holders.

Refer to the Piecing Diagram given with each block for assembly ideas.

Diamonds & Rust

Fabric & Piece Requirements

• 2 M31 light blue mottled
• 6 M31 orange print
• 4 M35 aqua solid (reverse 2 for M35R)
• 4 T11 aqua solid
• 2 T16 aqua solid
• 1 - 2" x 36" strip orange print for binding

Instructions

1. Sew a light blue M31 between two orange M31 and add M35 to one end and T11 to the other end to make a diagonal row as shown in Figure 1; press seams toward darker fabric. Repeat to make two rows.

Figure 1

2. Sew T11 and M35R to an orange M31 and add T16 to make a corner unit as shown in Figure 2; press seams away from M31. Repeat to make two corner units.

Figure 2

3. Join the rows and corner units to complete the pieced block; press seams in one direction.

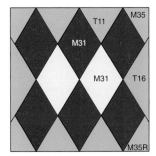

Diamonds & Rust
Placement Diagram
8" x 8"

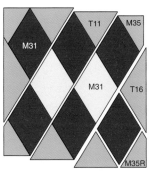

Piecing Diagram

Brilliance

Fabric & Piece Requirements

• 2 M31 orange print
• 2 T11 each aqua solid and orange tonal
• 4 T14 fuchsia solid (reverse 2 for T14R)
• 4 - 1¼" x 6½" A peach mottled
• 2 - 1¼" x 8½" B aqua print
• 1 - 2" x 36" strip orange print for binding

Instructions

1. Sew an orange T11 to an aqua T11 as shown in Figure 3; press seam toward darker fabric. Repeat to make two T11 units.

Figure 3

2. Sew a T11 unit to M31 to make an M31 unit; press seam toward M31. Repeat to make two M31 units.

3. Join the M31 units to complete the pieced center; press seam in one direction.

4. Center and stitch A to one side of the pieced center as shown in Figure 4; press seam toward A and trim ends even with the edges of the pieced center, again referring to Figure 4. Continue adding A all around the pieced center, pressing and trimming each strip after stitching.

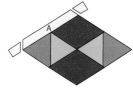

Figure 4

5. Sew T14 and T14R pieces to the pieced unit; press seams toward T14 and T14R.

6. Sew a B strip to the long sides of the pieced unit to complete the pieced block; press seams toward B.

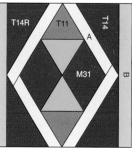

Brilliance
Placement Diagram
8" x 8"

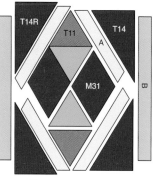

Piecing Diagram

Time Will Tell

Special occasions are time for family gatherings where food is most always the main attraction.

Project Notes

Cut pieces as listed either using a rotary cutter and rotary ruler or the templates from those starting on page 87.

Refer to the General Instructions for a list of basic sewing supplies and tools needed and for instructions to finish your pot holders.

Refer to the Piecing Diagram given with each block for assembly ideas.

Time Tunnel

Fabric & Piece Requirements

- 2 T19 each green and blue solids
- 4 S12 green solid
- 1 - 1½" x 6½" A each red and black prints, green tonal and rust solid
- 4 - 2" x 5½" B strips yellow stripe
- 1 - 2" x 36" strip brown print for binding

Instructions

1. Sew a green T19 to a blue T19; press seam toward darker fabric. Repeat to make two T19 units. Join the two units to complete the center unit as shown in Figure 1; press seam in one direction.

Figure 1

2. Center and sew an A strip to each side of the center, mitering corners referring to the General Instructions.

3. Sew B to opposite sides of the pieced unit; press seams toward B.

4. Sew S12 to each end of each remaining B strip; press seams toward B.

5. Sew a B-S12 unit to the remaining side of the pieced unit to complete the pieced block.

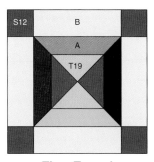

Time Tunnel
Placement Diagram
8" x 8"

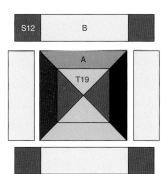

Piecing Diagram

Get-Together

Fabric & Piece Requirements

- 2 T2 each peach and rose prints
- 4 T20 gray print
- 4 T29 yellow print
- 4 - 2¼" x 4⅜" A brown mottled
- 4 - ¾" x 4¾" B black print
- 1 - 2" x 36" strip burgundy print for binding

Instructions

1. Sew a peach T2 to a red T2; press seam toward darker fabric. Repeat to make two units; join the units to complete the center unit. Press seam in one direction.

2. Center and sew B to T20; press seam toward T20. Repeat to make four B-T20 units. Trim the ends of B even with the edges of T20 as shown in Figure 2.

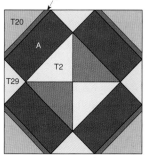
Figure 2

3. Add A to two B-T20 units; press seams away from A. Repeat to make two A-B-T20 corner units.

4. Sew an A-B-T20 corner unit to opposite sides of the center unit; press seams toward corner units.

5. Sew T29 to each end of each remaining A; press seam toward T29.

6. Add a B-T20 unit to each A-T29 unit to complete the side corner units; press seams away from A-T29.

7. Sew a side corner unit to opposite sides of the center row to complete the pieced block; press seams toward the side corner units.

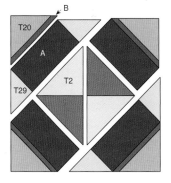

Get-Together
Placement Diagram
8" x 8"

Piecing Diagram

Family Dinner

Fabric & Piece Requirements
- 4 T18 each blue and rust solids
- 4 - 1½" x 4" each red print A and tan tonal B
- 4 - 1½" x 7½" C burgundy/cream check
- 1 - 2" x 36" strip burgundy solid for binding

Instructions
1. Sew a rust T18 to a blue T18 along the diagonal to make a T18 unit; press seam toward the darker fabric. Repeat to make four T18 units.
2. Join the four T18 units referring to the Piecing Diagram to complete the block center; press seams in one direction.
3. Sew B to A on the short ends; press seams toward A. Repeat to make four A-B units.
4. Center and sew an A-B unit to the block center, mitering corners referring to the General Instructions; press seams toward A-B units.
5. Sew a C strip to each side of the pieced center using partial seams referring to the General Instructions to complete the pieced top.

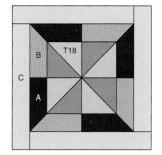

Family Dinner
Placement Diagram
8" x 8"

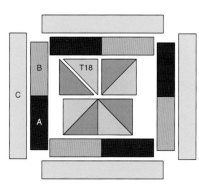

Piecing Diagram

Stop & Visit

Fabric & Piece Requirements
- 4 T18 each rust solid and red print
- 4 S10 green tonal
- 4 - 1¼" x 4" each tan tonal A and black print B
- 4 - 1¾" x 6" C burgundy/cream check
- 1 - 2" x 36" strip burgundy print for binding

Instructions
1. Sew a red T18 to a rust T18 to make a T18 unit; press seam toward darker fabric. Repeat to make four T18 units.

2. Sew A to the red T18 side and B to the rust T18 side of one T18 unit, matching on one square end as shown in Figure 3 and mitering corners referring to the General Instructions; press seams toward A and B. Repeat to make four A-B-T18 units.

Figure 3

3. Join two A-B-T18 units to make a row; press seams in one direction. Repeat to make two rows. Join the rows to complete the block center; press seams in one direction.
4. Sew C to two opposite sides of the block center; press seams toward C.
5. Sew S10 to each end of each remaining C strip; press seams toward C.
6. Sew a C-S10 unit to the remaining sides of the block center to complete the pieced block; press seams toward the C-S10 units.

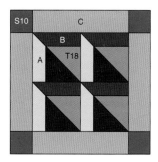

Stop & Visit
Placement Diagram
8" x 8"

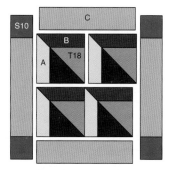

Piecing Diagram

A Little Fishy

Pieced fish designs in contemporary colors are fun to stitch.

Project Notes

Cut pieces as listed either using a rotary cutter and rotary ruler or the templates from those starting on page 87.

Refer to the General Instructions for a list of basic sewing supplies and tools needed and for instructions to finish your pot holders.

Refer to the Piecing Diagram given with each block for assembly ideas.

Polka-Dot Fish

Fabric & Piece Requirements

- 1 M3 fuchsia solid
- 1 M29 each red and orange prints
- 4 T4 each orange print and blue mottled
- 2 T5 blue mottled (reverse 1 for T5R)
- 2 T12 blue mottled
- 4 T27 blue mottled
- 1 - 4¼" x 4½" A orange solid
- 2 - 1" x 2" B blue mottled
- 1 - 1" x 1½" C gold tonal
- 4 - 1½" x 4" D blue mottled
- 2 - 1" x 9½" E fuchsia tonal
- 2 - 1" x 7½" F fuchsia tonal
- Scrap yellow print for appliquéd circles
- 1 - 2" x 40" strip black check for binding
- Dark blue embroidery floss

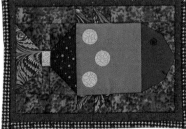

Instructions

1. Cut, prepare and stitch circle pieces to A using pattern given on page 91 and referring to the General Instructions and the block drawing.

2. Sew T12 to M3 and add T5 and T5R to complete the head unit; press seams away from M3.

3. Sew T27 to each M29 to complete two T-M units; press seams toward T27.

4. Sew B to each short side of C; press seams toward B.

5. Sew the B-C unit between the two T-M units to complete the tail unit.

6. Join the head unit and the tail unit with A to complete the fish unit as shown in Figure 1; press seams toward A.

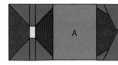

Figure 1

7. Sew an orange T4 to a blue T4 to complete a T4 unit; press seam toward darker fabric. Repeat to make four T4 units.

8. Join two T4 units and add D to each end to make a top strip; press seams toward D. Repeat to make the bottom strip.

9. Sew the top and bottom strips to the fish unit; press seams away from the fish unit.

10. Sew E to opposite long sides and F to the short ends of the pieced unit to complete the pieced block; press seams toward E and F.

11. Stem-stitch and satin-stitch eye and mouth using 2 strands dark blue embroidery floss to finish.

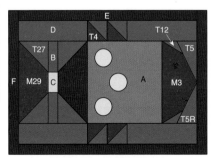

Polka-Dot Fish
Placement Diagram
10" x 7"

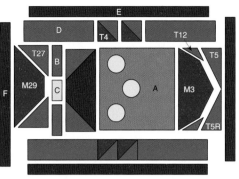

Piecing Diagram

Friendly Shark

Fabric & Piece Requirements

- 1 M3 lavender solid
- 2 M29 lavender solid
- 4 T4 each lavender solid and blue print
- 2 T5 blue print (reverse 1 for T5R)
- 2 T12 blue print
- 2 T27 blue print
- 2 T33 each blue print and aqua solid
- 1 - 3¼" x 4½" A lavender solid
- 2 - 1" x 2" B blue print
- 1 - 1" x 1½" C lavender solid
- 4 - 1½" x 4" D blue print
- 2 - 1" x 9½" E gold check
- 2 - 1" x 7½" F gold check
- 1 - 2" x 40" strip black check for binding
- Purple embroidery floss

Instructions

1. Sew T12 to M3 and add T5 and T5R to complete the head unit; press seams away from M3.

2. Sew a lavender T4 to a blue T4 to make a T4 unit; press seam toward darker fabric. Repeat to make eight T4 units.

American School of Needlework · Berne, Indiana 46711 · DRGnetwork.com

3. Join four T4 units to make a fin strip referring to Figure 2; press seams in one direction.

Figure 2

4. Sew two T27 pieces to one M29 to complete a T-M unit; press seams toward T27.

5. Sew a blue T33 to an aqua T33 to complete a T33 unit; press seam toward darker fabric. Repeat to make a reversed T33 unit.

6. Sew the T33 and reverse T33 units to the remaining M29 to complete an M-T unit; press seams toward M29.

7. Sew B to each short side of C; press seams toward B.

8. Sew the B-C unit between the T-M and the M-T units to complete a tail unit as shown in Figure 3; press seams toward the B-C unit.

Figure 3

9. Join the head unit, fin strip and tail unit with A to complete the fish unit as shown in Figure 4; press seams toward A.

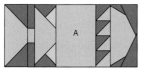

Figure 4

10. Complete the block referring to steps 8–11 for the Polka Dot Fish except use 2 strands purple embroidery floss for eye and mouth to finish.

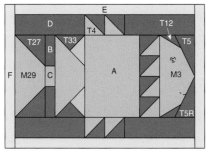

Friendly Shark
Placement Diagram
10" x 7"

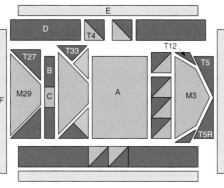

Piecing Diagram

Tropical Fish

Fabric & Piece Requirements
- 1 M3 orange tonal
- 1 M29 each orange and blue tonals and fuchsia solid
- 2 S9 lavender solid
- 2 T5 blue tonal (reverse 1 for T5R)
- 2 T12 blue tonal
- 2 T27 orange tonal
- 4 T27 blue tonal
- 1 - 3¼" x 4½" A fuchsia solid
- 2 - 1½" x 4" B blue tonal
- 2 - 1½" x 5" C blue tonal
- 2 - 1" x 9½" D purple print
- 2 - 1" x 7½" E purple print
- Scrap aqua print for appliqué
- 1 - 2" x 40" strip gold tonal for binding
- Dark blue embroidery floss

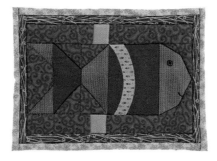

Instructions
1. Cut, prepare and stitch fish stripe piece to A using pattern given on page 91 and referring to the General Instructions and the block drawing.

2. Sew T12 to M3 and add T5 and T5R to complete the head unit; press seams away from M3.

3. Sew orange T27 to each end of one M29 to complete a T-M unit; press seams toward T27.

4. Repeat step 3 with blue T27 pieces and the remaining M29 pieces to make two M-T units.

5. Join the T-M and M-T units as shown in Figure 5 to complete the tail unit; press seams in one direction.

Figure 5

6. Join the head unit and the tail unit with A to complete the fish unit referring to the Piecing Diagram; press seams toward A.

7. Sew S9 between one each B and C to make a top strip; press seams away from S9. Repeat to make a bottom strip.

8. Sew the top and bottom strips to the fish unit; press seams away from the fish unit.

9. Sew D to opposite long sides and E to the short ends of the pieced unit to complete the pieced block; press seams toward D and E.

10. Stem-stitch and satin-stitch eye and mouth using 2 strands dark blue embroidery floss to finish.

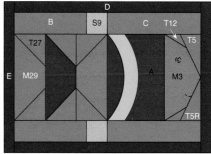

Tropical Fish
Placement Diagram
10" x 7"

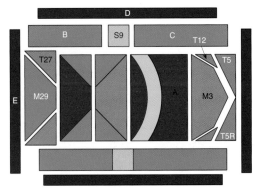

Piecing Diagram

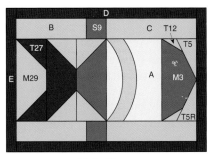

Fish Story
Placement Diagram
10" x 7"

Fish Story

Fabric & Piece Requirements
- 1 M3 purple tonal
- 1 M29 each purple tonal and aqua and purple prints
- 2 S9 blue mottled
- 2 T5 aqua print (reverse 1 for T5R)
- 2 T12 aqua print
- 2 T27 purple print
- 4 T27 aqua print
- 1 - 3¼" x 4½" A yellow print
- 2 - 1½" x 4" B aqua print
- 2 - 1½" x 5" C aqua print

- 2 - 1" x 9½" D red print
- 2 - 1" x 7½" E red print
- Scrap lavender solid for appliqué
- 1 - 2" x 40" strip rose print for binding
- Yellow embroidery floss

Instructions
1. Refer to Tropical Fish instructions to complete the Fish Story block referring to the Piecing Diagram for color placement of pieces except use 2 strands yellow embroidery floss for eye and mouth to finish.

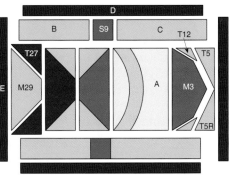

Piecing Diagram

Lazy Hazy Days

Stitch up some pot holders as reminders of those warm, lazy days of summer.

Project Notes
Cut pieces as listed either using a rotary cutter and rotary ruler or the templates from those starting on page 87.
Refer to the General Instructions for a list of basic sewing supplies and tools needed and for instructions to finish your pot holders.
Refer to the Piecing Diagram given with each block for assembly ideas.

Summer Sun

Fabric & Piece Requirements
- 8 M4 aqua solid (reverse 4 for M4R)
- 4 S9 fuchsia solid
- 12 T4 each aqua check and orange print
- 8 T9 gold tonal
- 4 - 1½" x 3½" A aqua check
- 1 - 2" x 36" strip turquoise solid for binding
- 4" x 5" piece fusible web and gold tonal for sun rays

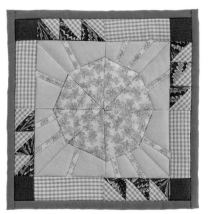

American School of Needlework • Berne, Indiana 46711 • DRGnetwork.com

Instructions

1. Bond fusible web to the wrong side of the gold tonal strip; cut (11) ¼" x 2" ray pieces from the fused strip. Remove paper backing.

2. Arrange and fuse one or two ray pieces to each M4 and M4R piece referring to the Placement Diagram for positioning; trim excess at edges. Machine-zigzag-stitch along edges to hold in place.

3. Sew M4 to T9; press seam toward M4. Repeat to make four M-T and four reverse M-T units.

4. Join one each M-T and reverse M-T units to make a quarter unit; press seam in one direction. Repeat to complete four quarter units.

5. Sew an orange T4 to an aqua T4 to make a T4 unit; press seam toward darker fabric. Repeat to make 12 T4 units.

6. Join three T4 units to make a T4 strip; press seams in one direction. Repeat to make four T4 strips.

7. Sew a T4 strip to the M4 side of each quarter unit; press seams toward M4.

8. Sew S9 to A; press seam toward S9. Repeat to make four A-S9 strips.

9. Sew an A-S9 strip to the M4R side of each quarter unit to complete a block quarter. Repeat to complete four block quarters.

10. Join two block quarters to make a row; press seam in one direction. Repeat to make two rows.

11. Join the rows to complete the pieced block; press seam in one direction.

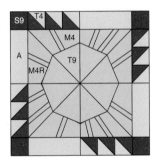

Summer Sun
Placement Diagram
8" x 8"

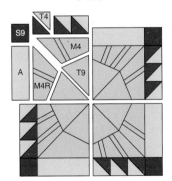

Piecing Diagram

Summer Blooms

Fabric & Piece Requirements
- 3 T1 each light green mottled and fuchsia solid
- 7 T1 dark green print
- 14 T4 light green mottled
- 3 T18 fuchsia solid
- 8 - 1½" x 2½" A light green mottled
- 2 - 1" x 7½" B light green mottled
- 4 - 1" x 8" C gold tonal
- 1 - 2" x 36" strip purple print for binding
- Green and rose embroidery floss

Instructions
1. Sew a green T1 to a fuchsia T1 to make a T1 unit; press seam toward darker fabric. Repeat to make three T1 units.

2. Sew a T1 unit to each T18 to complete three T units; press seams toward T18.

3. Sew T4 to each short side of T1; press seam toward T1. Repeat to make seven T1-T4 units.

4. Join two T1-T4 units with three A pieces and one T unit to make a two-leaf flower row; press seams toward A. Repeat for two two-leaf flower rows.

5. Repeat step 4 with three T1-T4 units and two A pieces to make a three-leaf flower row; press seams toward A.

6. Join the rows with B referring to the Piecing Diagram to complete the pieced center; press seams toward B.

7. Sew a C strip to each side of the pieced center using partial seams referring to the General Instructions.

8. Stem-stitch stem lines using 2 strands green embroidery floss and flower centers using 2 strands rose embroidery floss to complete the pieced block.

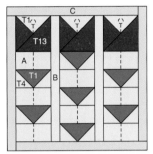

Summer Blooms
Placement Diagram
8" x 8"

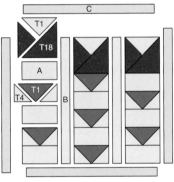

Piecing Diagram

Sailboat

Fabric & Piece Requirements
- 1 T26 white solid
- 1 T26R blue mottled
- 2 T26 aqua solid (reverse 1 for T26R)
- 2 - 1½" x 3¼" A aqua solid
- 1 - 3" x 6" B blue tonal
- 2 - 1" x 6½" C yellow print
- 2 - 1" x 8½" D yellow print
- 2 - 1" x 7½" E lavender solid
- 2 - 1" x 9½" F lavender solid
- Red solid scrap for boat appliqué
- 1 - 2" x 40" strip turquoise solid for binding
- Yellow embroidery floss

    American School of Needlework • Berne, Indiana 46711 • DRGnetwork.com

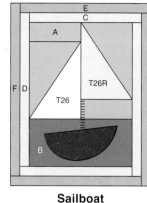

Sailboat
Placement Diagram
7½" x 9½"

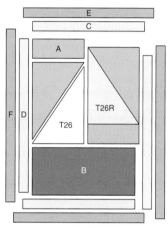

Piecing Diagram

Instructions

1. Cut, prepare and stitch the boat piece to B using pattern given on page 95 and referring to the General Instructions and the block drawing.

2. Sew a white T26 to an aqua T26 to make a T26 unit; press seam toward darker fabric. Repeat with T26R blue and aqua pieces to make a T26R unit; press seam toward darker fabric.

3. Sew A to the aqua end of the T26 unit and the blue end of the T26R unit to complete the sail units; press seams toward A.

4. Join the sail units referring to the Piecing Diagram to complete the sail/sky unit; press seam in one direction.

5. Sew the appliquéd B piece to the sail/sky unit to complete the pieced center; press seam toward B.

6. Sew C and D strips and then the E and F strips to the pieced center using partial seams referring to the Piecing Diagram and the General Instructions; press seams toward C, D, E and F.

7. Connect the sail and the boat with two rows of stem stitches using 2 strands of yellow embroidery floss. Add straight stitches perpendicular to the stem-stitched rows to finish.

Seaside Shade

Fabric & Piece Requirements

- Assorted 1"–2"-wide 7"-long strips orange/fuchsia scraps for A
- 2 - 1½" x 6½" B lavender solid
- 2 - 1½" x 8½" C lavender solid
- Scraps blue and purple prints and black solid for appliqué
- 1 - 2" x 36" strip turquoise solid for binding

Instructions

1. Join the assorted A pieces and trim to 6½" x 6½".

2. Sew B to the top and bottom and C to opposite sides of A; press seams toward B and C.

3. Cut, prepare and stitch the umbrella appliqué pieces to A using patterns given on page 95 and referring to the General Instructions and the Placement Diagram to complete the block.

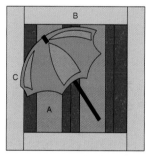

Seaside Shade
Placement Diagram
8" x 8"

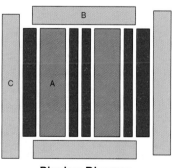

Piecing Diagram

Holiday Fun

Say "Happy Holidays" with the perfect hostess gift at any holiday gathering using these fun holiday pot holders.

Project Notes

Cut pieces as listed either using a rotary cutter and rotary ruler or the templates from those starting on page 87.

Refer to the General Instructions for a list of basic sewing supplies and tools needed and for instructions to finish your pot holders.

Refer to the Piecing Diagram given with each block for assembly ideas.

Mr. Snowman

Fabric & Piece Requirements

• Scraps white, tan and black solid for appliqué
• 1 - 4½" x 7" A red print
• 2 - 1¾" x 4½" B green solid
• 2 - 1¾" x 9½" C green solid
• 2 - 1" x 9½" D red/green stripe
• 1 - 2" x 40" strip cream print for binding
• Black and blue embroidery floss

Instructions

1. Sew B to opposite short sides of A; press seams toward B.

2. Sew C and D to opposite long sides of the A-B unit to complete the block background; press seams toward C and D.

3. Cut, prepare and stitch snowman appliqué pieces to the block background using patterns given on page 95 and referring to the General Instructions and the Placement Diagram.

4. Stem-stitch mouth and add French-knot eyes using 2 strands black embroidery floss. Using 2 strands blue embroidery floss and a running stitch, stitch along center of hatband to finish.

Mr. Snowman
Placement Diagram
7½" x 9"

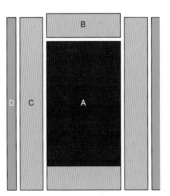

Piecing Diagram

Candy Cane

Fabric & Piece Requirements

• 1 M23 burgundy solid
• 4 T18 green tonal
• 2 - 1¾" x 4½" A dark green print
• 2 - 1¾" x 9½" B dark green print
• 2 - 1" x 9½" C green print
• Scrap fusible web, white and red solids for appliqué
• 1 - 2" x 40" strip cream/burgundy print for binding

Instructions

1. Sew T18 to each short side of M23 to complete the pieced center; press seams toward T18.

2. Sew A to the top and bottom and B and C to opposite long sides of the pieced center; press seams toward A, B and C.

3. Cut, prepare and stitch candy-cane appliqué piece to the pieced center using pattern given on page 95 and referring to the General Instructions and the Placement Diagram.

American School of Needlework • Berne, Indiana 46711 • DRGnetwork.com

4. Trace the candy cane stripe patterns on the paper side of fusible scrap. Bond fusible web to the wrong side of the red solid; cut out stripe pieces on traced lines. Remove paper backing.

5. Position the stripes on the candy cane; fuse in place. Machine-satin-stitch in place using thread to match fabric to finish.

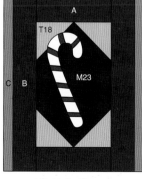

Candy Cane
Placement Diagram
7½" x 9"

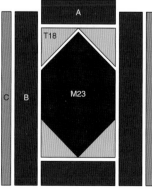

Piecing Diagram

Fir Tree

Fabric & Piece Requirements

- 2 M15 green tonal
- 2 M28 white solid (reverse 1 for M28R)
- 1 S9 dark green print
- 1 T15 red/black print
- 2 T27 white solid
- 4 T31 white solid
- 1 T34 green tonal
- 1 - 1" x 4½" A red print
- 2 - 1½" x 2" B white solid
- 2 - 1¾" x 4½" C green solid
- 2 - 1¾" x 9½" D green solid
- 2 - 1" x 9½" E red/green stripe
- 1 - 2" x 40" strip tan print for binding

Instructions

1. Sew T31 to each short side of each M15 to make a T-M unit; press seam toward M15. Repeat to make two T-M units.
2. Join the two T-M units and add A; press seams toward A.
3. Sew B to each side of S9 to make the trunk unit; press seams toward S9.
4. Sew the trunk unit to the A side of the A-T-M unit to complete the tree-bottom unit; press seam toward A.
5. Sew T15 to the end of M28; press seam toward T15. Add T27 to complete a corner unit; press seam toward T27.

6. Sew T27 to M28R to complete the reverse corner unit; press seam toward T27.
7. Sew the corner and reverse corner units to T34 to complete the tree-top unit; press seams toward T34.
8. Sew the tree-top unit to the tree-bottom unit to complete the pieced center; press seam in one direction.
9. Sew C to the top and bottom of the pieced center; press seams toward C.
10. Sew D and R to opposite long sides of the pieced center to complete the pieced block; press seams toward D and E.

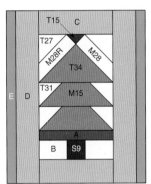

Fir Tree
Placement Diagram
7½" x 9"

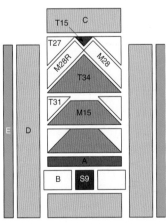

Piecing Diagram

Noel Stocking

Fabric & Piece Requirements

- 1 M13 red print
- 1 M14 green solid
- 1 S9 green solid
- 1 T4 green solid
- 1 - 1½" x 7½" A red/black print
- 1 - 1½" x 7⅝" B red print
- 1 - 1½" x 6½" C red/black print
- 1 - 1½" x 6⅝" D red print
- 1 - 2½" x 4½" E white solid
- 1 - 2" x 7⅝" F green solid
- 2 - 1½" x 9½" G green solid
- 1 - 2" x 40" strip tan print for binding

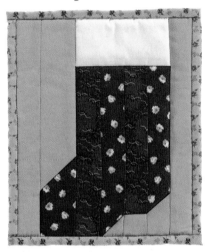

Instructions

1. Trim B, D and F strips at a 45-degree angle on one end as shown in Figure 1.

Figure 1

2. Sew T4 to the angled end of B, S9 to one end of C and M14 to the angled end of D; press seams toward darker fabrics.
3. Join the pieced strips with A referring to the Piecing Diagram to make the stocking-body unit; press seams in one direction.
4. Sew E to the top edge of the stocking-body unit; press seam away from E.

5. Sew M13 to the angled end of F; press seam toward M13. Sew the F-M13 unit to the A side of the stocking-body unit; press seam toward F-M13.

6. Sew G to opposite long sides of the pieced unit to complete the pieced block; press seams toward G.

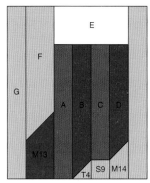

Noel Stocking
Placement Diagram
7½" x 9"

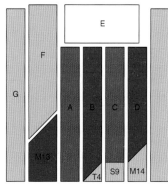

Piecing Diagram

Snow Time

Fabric & Piece Requirements
• 2 S7 cream solid
• 4 T25 each red print and black solid
• 2 - 1½" x 3½" each light green tonal A and red print C
• 2 - 1½" x 4½" each red print B and light green tonal D
• 1 - 2" x 36" strip tan print for binding
• Light blue and light green embroidery floss

Instructions

1. Sew a red T25 to a black T25; press seam toward darker fabric. Repeat to make four T25 units.

2. Join two T25 units to make a T25 square; press seam in one direction. Repeat to make two T25 squares.

3. Cut, prepare and stitch mitten appliqué pieces to S7 using patterns given on page 96 and referring to the General Instructions and the Placement Diagram.

4. Sew A to the black side and D to the red side of each T18 unit; press seams toward A and D.

5. Sew C to the outer hand side and B to the top or bottom of each appliquéd S7 square; press seam toward C and B.

6. Join the pieced units in two rows of two units each referring to the Piecing Diagram; press seams in opposite directions.

7. Join the pieced rows to complete the pieced block; press seam in one direction.

8. Straight-stitch lines at the bottom of the each mitten using 2 strands light green embroidery floss.

9. Stem-stitch the snowflake design given in the center of each T25 unit using 2 strands light blue embroidery floss.

Snowflake Pattern

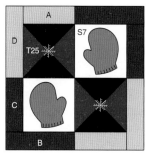

Snow Time
Placement Diagram
8" x 8"

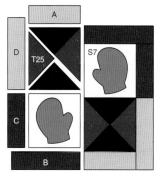

Piecing Diagram

Holiday Wreath

Fabric & Piece Requirements
• 1 M24 peach mottled
• 4 M17 green print
• 4 M18 green print
• 4 T17 green solid
• 4 T27 each green solid and peach mottled
• 4 - 1½" x 7½" A red/black print
• 4" x 4" scrap red solid and fusible web for appliqué
• 1 - 2" x 36" strip tan print for binding

Instructions

1. Sew T17 to each angled side of M24 to complete the block center; press seams toward T17.

2. Sew M17 to each side of the block center as shown in Figure 2; press seams toward M17.

3. Sew a green T27 to each corner of the block center, again referring to Figure 2; press seams toward T27.

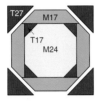

Figure 2

4. Sew M18 to each side of the block center; press seams toward M18.

5. Sew a peach T27 to each corner of the block center to complete the pieced center; press seams toward T27.

6. Sew an A strip to each side of the pieced center using partial seams referring to the General Instructions to complete the block piecing.

7. Trace the bow design given on page 95 onto the paper side of the fusible square. Bond fusible web to the wrong side of the square of red solid; cut out bow shape on traced lines. Remove paper backing.

8. Position the bow on the pieced center; fuse in place. Machine-satin-stitch in place using thread to match fabric to finish.

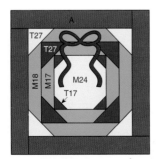

Holiday Wreath
Placement Diagram
8" x 8"

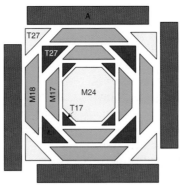

Piecing Diagram

Gift Surprise

Fabric & Piece Requirements
- 2 M17 red tonal
- 2 M18 red print
- 4 M25 white solid (reverse 2 for M25R)
- 4 M26 white solid (reverse 2 for M26R)
- 2 T19 white solid
- 12 T27 green metallic
- 4 - 1½" x 7½" A strips dark green solid
- 1 - 2" x 36" strip green metallic for binding

Instructions

1. Sew T27 to each short side of T19; press seams toward T27.

2. Add M17 to the T27 side of the pieced unit; press seam toward M17.

3. Add M25 and M25R to the short ends of the pieced unit as shown in Figure 3; press seams toward the M25 pieces.

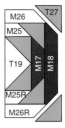

Figure 3

4. Sew T27 to the angled edges of the pieced unit, again referring to Figure 3; press seams toward T27.

5. Repeat steps 2–4 with M18, M26 and T27 pieces to complete half the block. Repeat to make two halves and join on the M18 sides to complete the pieced center; press seams in one direction.

6. Sew an A strip to each side of the pieced center using partial seams referring to the General Instructions to complete the pieced block.

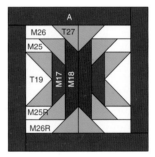

Gift Surprise
Placement Diagram
8" x 8"

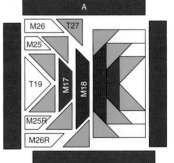

Piecing Diagram

Open Me First

Fabric & Piece Requirements
- 4 M26R red/green stripe
- 4 M26 red print
- 8 M25 light green mottled (reverse 4 for M25R)
- 4 S12 white solid
- 8 T27 green solid
- 4 - 1½" x 7½" A light green mottled
- 1 - 2" x 36" strip red print for binding

Instructions
1. Sew M25 and M25R to two adjacent sides of S12; add T27. Press seams away from S12.
2. Add M20 and M20R and T27 to the pieced unit to complete a block quarter; press seams away from S12. Repeat to make four block quarters.
3. Join the pieced block quarters referring to the Piecing Diagram to complete the pieced center, pressing seams in rows in opposite directions and then in one direction.
4. Sew an A strip to each side of the pieced center using partial seams referring to the General Instructions to complete the pieced block.

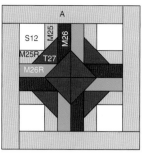

Open Me First
Placement Diagram
8" x 8"

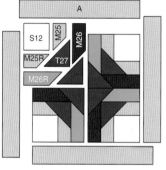

Piecing Diagram

Piecing & Appliqué Templates

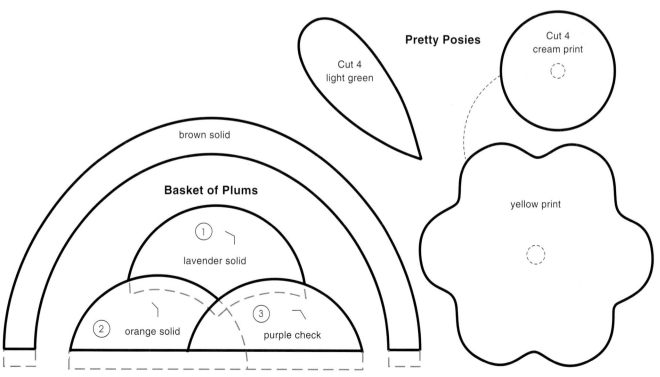

Pretty Posies

Cut 4
light green

Cut 4
cream print

yellow print

brown solid

Basket of Plums

① lavender solid

② orange solid

③ purple check

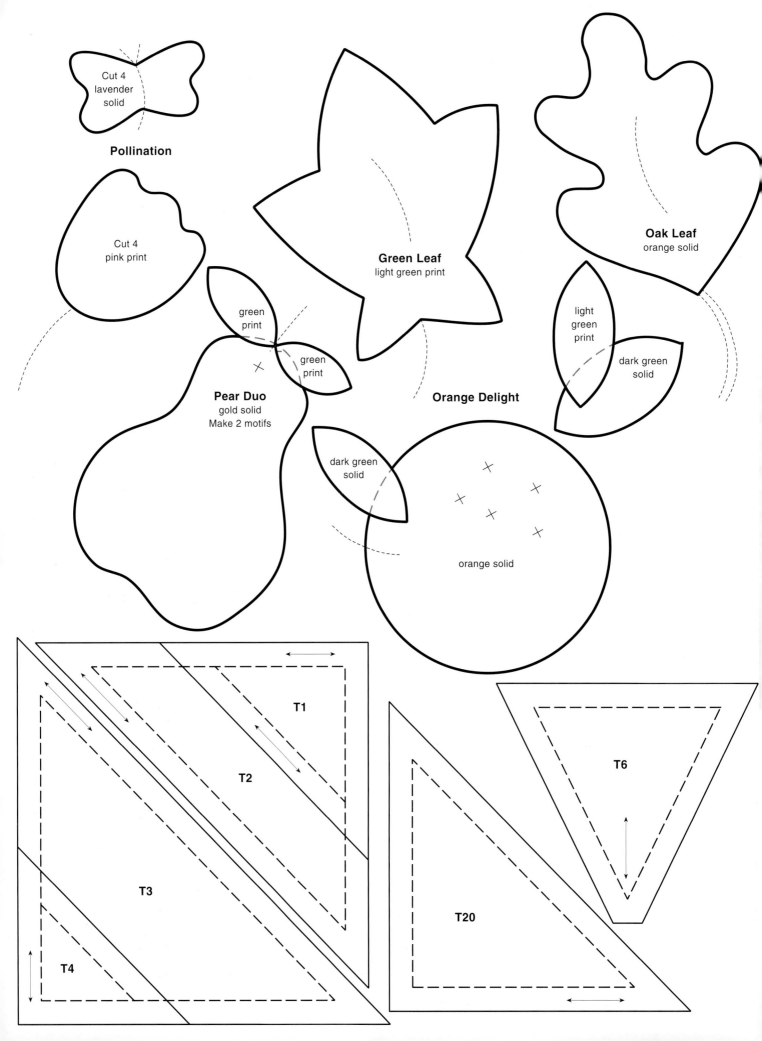

Cut 4
lavender
solid

Pollination

Cut 4
pink print

Green Leaf
light green print

Oak Leaf
orange solid

green
print

green
print

light
green
print

dark green
solid

Pear Duo
gold solid
Make 2 motifs

Orange Delight

dark green
solid

orange solid

T1

T2

T3

T4

T20

T6

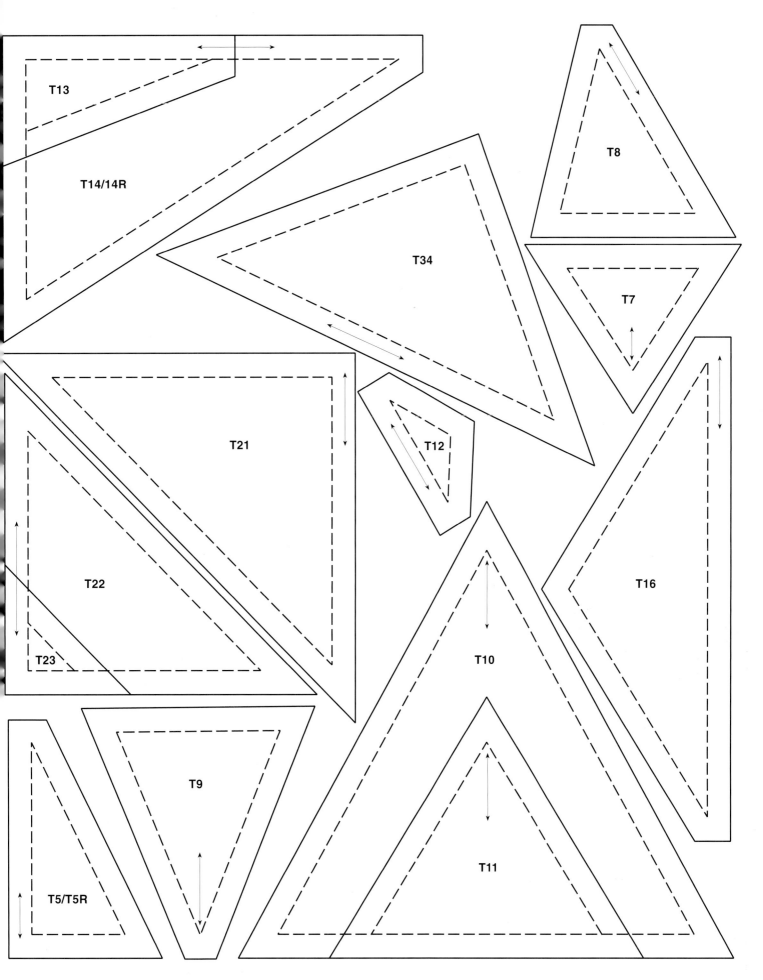

T13

T14/14R

T34

T8

T7

T21

T12

T16

T22

T23

T10

T9

T5/T5R

T11

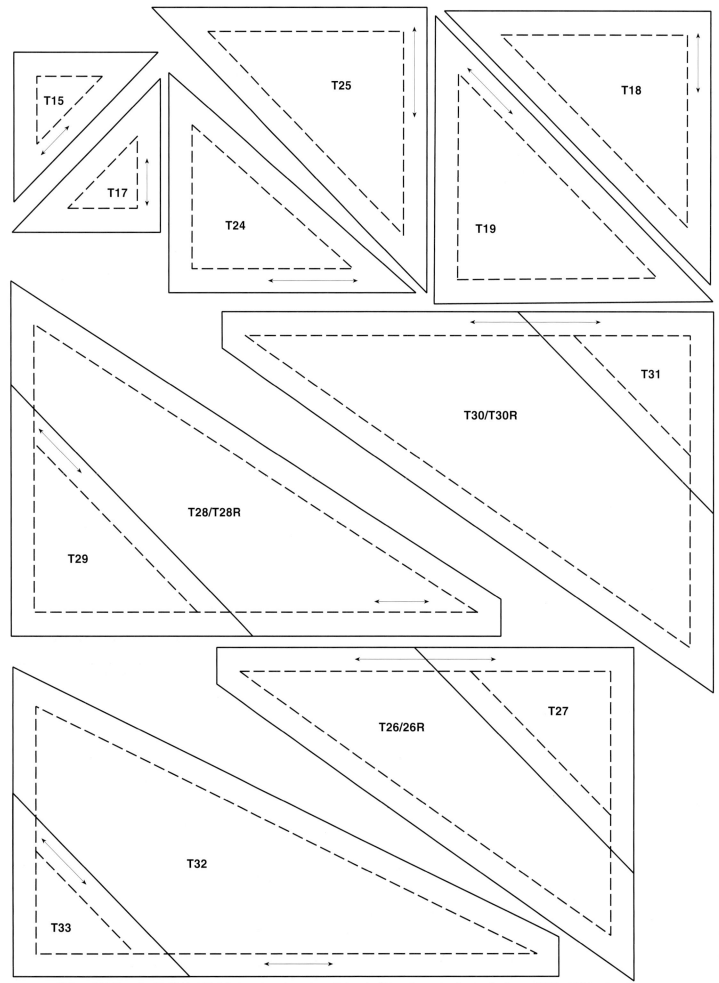

 American School of Needlework · Berne, Indiana 46711 · DRGnetwork.com

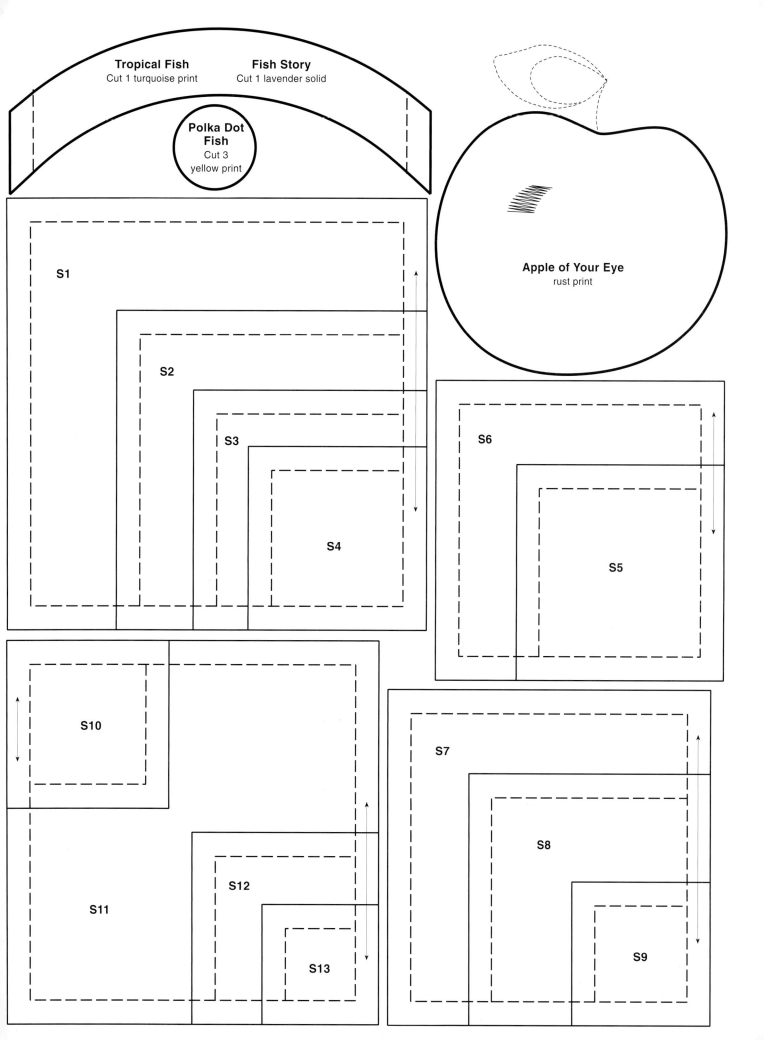

Tropical Fish
Cut 1 turquoise print

Fish Story
Cut 1 lavender solid

Polka Dot Fish
Cut 3 yellow print

Apple of Your Eye
rust print

S1

S2

S3

S4

S6

S5

S10

S11

S12

S13

S7

S8

S9

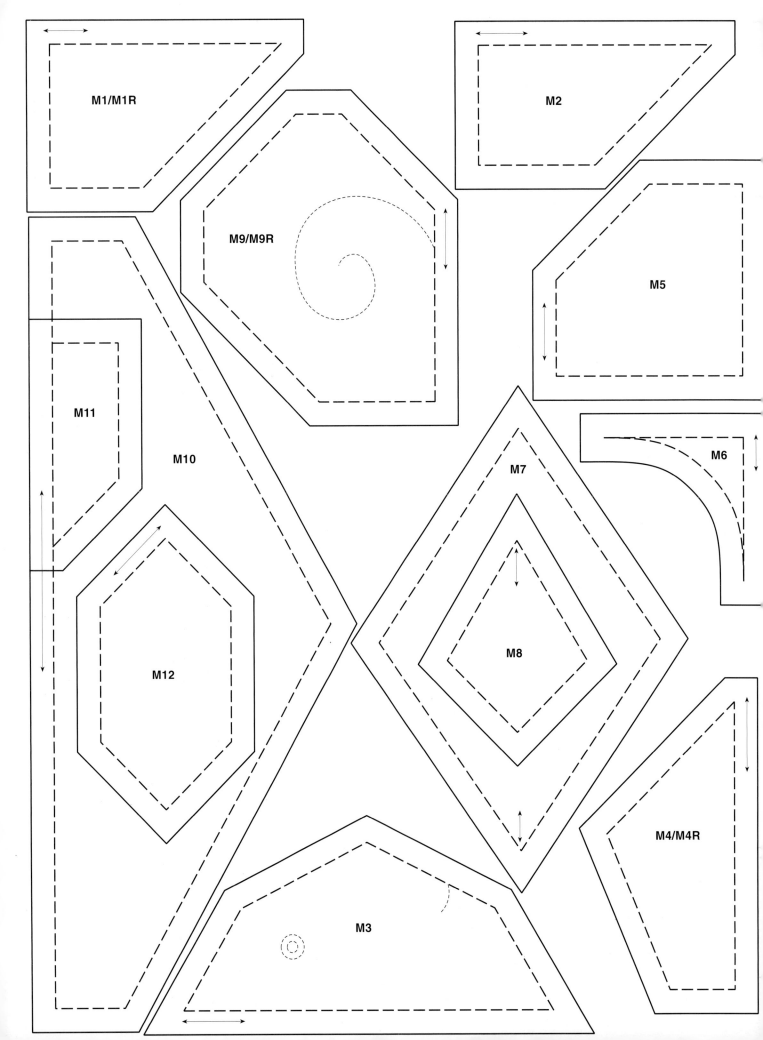

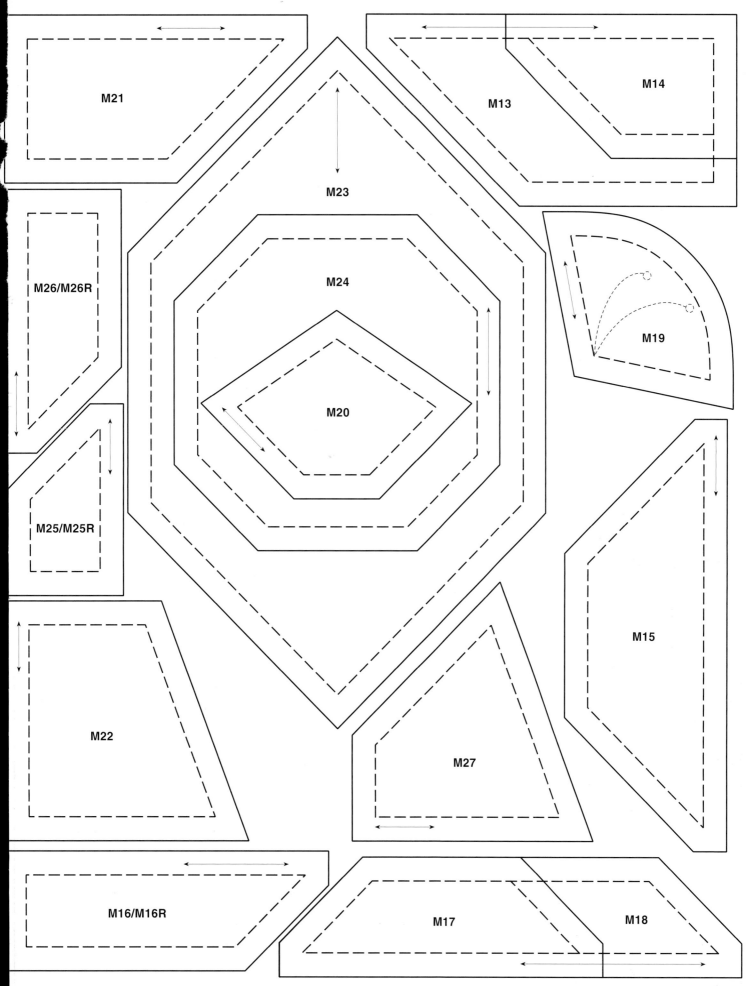

M21

M13   M14

M23

M26/M26R

M24

M19

M20

M25/M25R

M15

M22

M27

M16/16R

M17   M18

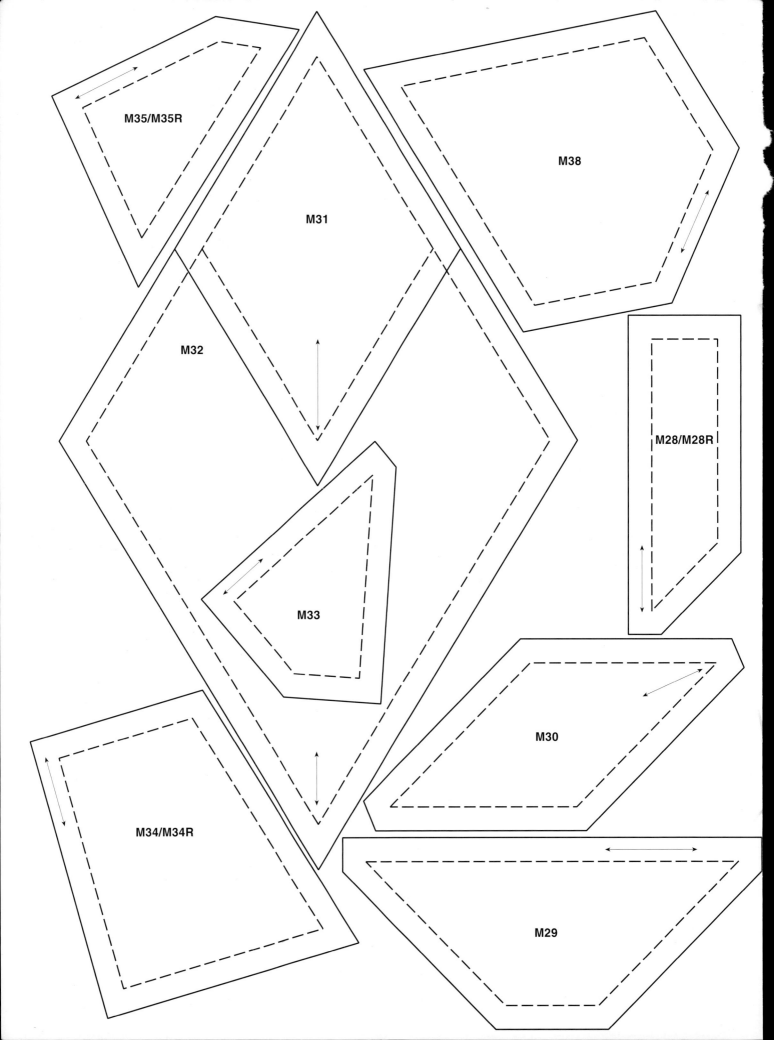

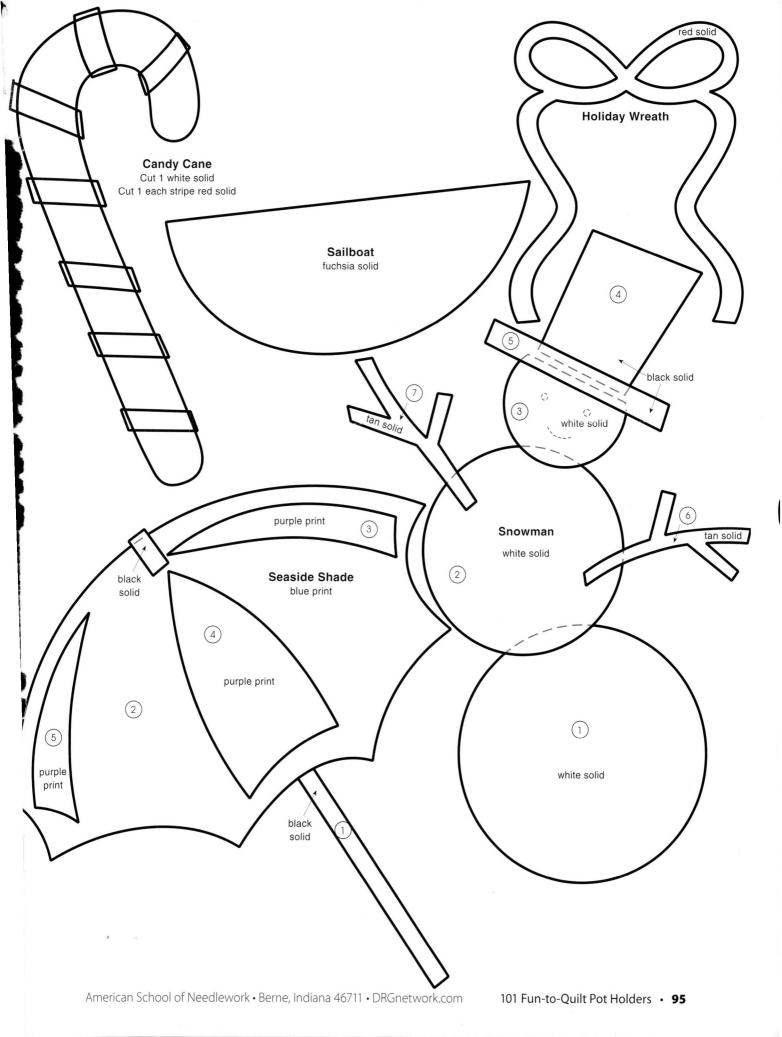

Candy Cane
Cut 1 white solid
Cut 1 each stripe red solid

Sailboat
fuchsia solid

Holiday Wreath
red solid

black solid

white solid

tan solid

Snowman
white solid

tan solid

Seaside Shade
blue print

purple print

black solid

purple print

purple print

white solid

black solid

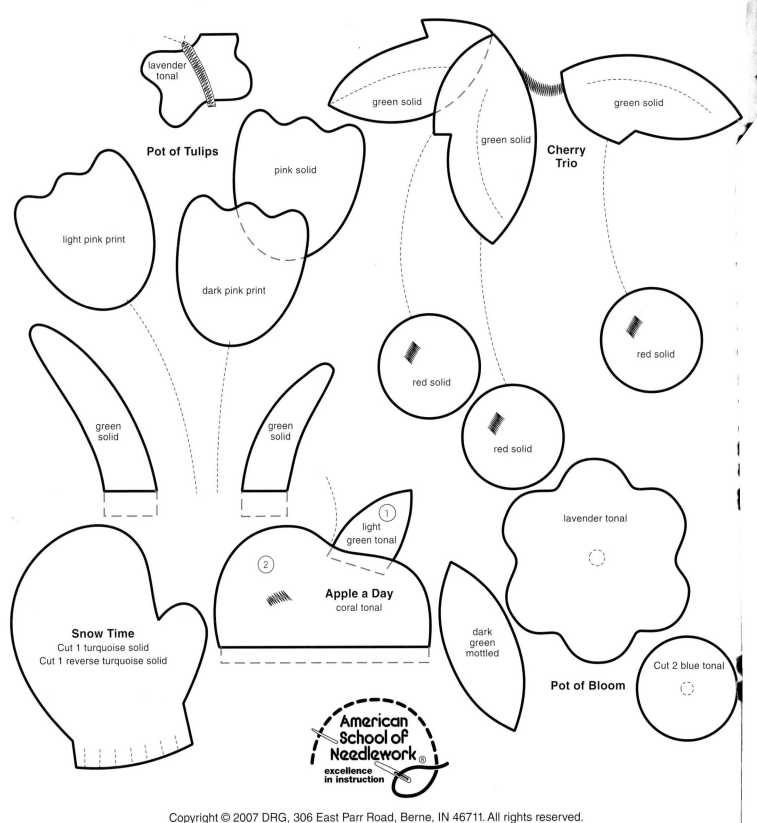

Pot of Tulips

lavender tonal

pink solid

light pink print

dark pink print

green solid

green solid

green solid

green solid

Cherry Trio

green solid

red solid

red solid

red solid

① light green tonal

② **Apple a Day**
coral tonal

lavender tonal

Snow Time
Cut 1 turquoise solid
Cut 1 reverse turquoise solid

dark green mottled

Pot of Bloom

Cut 2 blue tonal

American School of Needlework®
excellence in instruction

RETAIL STORES: If you would like to carry this pattern book or any other DRG publications, visit DRGwholesale.com.

Every effort has been made to ensure that the instructions in this publication are complete and accurate.
We cannot, however, take responsibility for human error, typographical mistakes or variations in individual work.
Please visit ClotildeCustomerCare.com to check for pattern updates.

ISBN: 978-1-59012-200-6   All rights reserved.   Printed in USA   11 12 13 14

LIbrary of Congress Control Number: 2007921615